Destined for Wealth

Destined for Wealth

Master the Art of a Prosperous Life

Larisa Olteanu
www.unshakablewealth.com

Published by Game Changer Publishing

Paperback ISBN: 978-1-961189-37-9
Hardcover ISBN: 978-1-961189-38-6
Digital ISBN: 978-1-961189-39-3

DEDICATION

To God, for creating me as His vessel to carry out His purpose. To my amazing husband Martin, who unconditionally supports every adventure. To my children, who are the best gift God could ever bless me with. To my mom and brother, who I am very grateful for.

Read This First!

Just to say thanks for buying and reading my book, I would like to give you a few free bonus gifts, no strings attached!

To Download Your Wealth Building Toolkit Now, Visit:
unshakablewealth.com/bookgifts

Take Our FREE Wealth-Building *90 Second* Quiz So I Can Hand Over Resources Specific To How YOU Want To Start Building Unshakable Wealth And a Prosperous Life:
unshakablewealth.com/wealthquiz

Attend Our FREE Wealth-Building Class:
unshakablewealth.com/class

Destined for Wealth

Master the Art of a Prosperous Life

Larisa Olteanu

www.GameChangerPublishing.com

"For I know the plans I have for you," declares the Lord, "plans to prosper you and not to harm you, plans to give you hope and a future."

- Jeremiah 29:11

Table of Contents

Introduction – The Power of Choice in Building a Prosperous Life 1

Phase 1 – Building a Wealth Foundation 7

Chapter 1 – The Unshakable Wealth Identity 9

1.1 – Establish Your New Wealth Identity 9

1.2 – Discover Your Unstoppable "Why" 19

1.3 – Secrets to Building Winning Habits 23

Chapter 2 – Conquering Your Dreams 33

2.1 – Shatter Limiting Beliefs and Dream Big 33

2.2 – Crafting Powerful SMART Goals for Wealth and Abundance .. 43

2.3 – Design a Progress-Tracking System 52

Chapter 3 – Fostering a Prosperous Mindset 59

3.1 – Harness the Power of Vision Boards for a Rich Life 59

3.2 – Embrace a Gratitude System for Lasting Fulfillment 63

3.3 – Cultivate an Effective Daily Success Routine 69

Phase 2 – Money Management System 73

Chapter 4 – Optimized Value-Based Spending 75

4.1 – Establish a money tracking system 75

4.2 – Ditch Traditional Budgeting for Value-Based Spending 78

4.3 – Align Spending with Core Values and Enjoy What Matters 81

Chapter 5 – The Super Savings Tactics 89

5.1 – Focus on Smart Savings and Uncover Hidden Opportunities ... 89

5.2 – Design a Strategic Accounts Structure 93

5.3 – Automate Your Money with the "Pay Yourself First" Model 97

5.4– Get Paid What You Are Worth 103

Phase 3 – Achieving Compounding Growth 109
Chapter 6 – The Ultimate Investing Secrets 111
6.1 – Calculate Your Dream Life Number 111
6.2 – Demystifying Investing and Its Potential 114
6.3 – Learn The Stock Market Investing 127
6.4 – Unlock the Power of Real Estate Passive Income 143
Chapter 7 – Embracing the Wealthy Life Plan 155
7.1– Estate Planning: Secure Your Legacy Like the Wealthy 155
7.2 – Optimize for Greater Freedom and Less Busy Work 162
Case Studies – Interviews With Everyday Millionaires 171
Resources 183

INTRODUCTION

The Power of Choice in Building a Prosperous Life

I was six years old, standing in our kitchen on Nicolae Costin Street, watching in horror how my drunken stepfather Alex dangled my mom outside the window of our fifth-floor apartment in Chisinau, Moldova. Gathering my courage, I edged closer and tried to calm him, just as I'd learned to do every other time he'd begun abusing her. Looking back at me, he paused and suddenly yelled, "You're lucky you have your daughter!" and yanked Mom back in.

Saving my mother's life was my first realization that life is all about choice: my stepfather's choice to end or sustain my mother's life, my choice to let my difficult childhood hold me back or use it as a building block to something better.

Thankfully, my mother and I eventually escaped Alex, and my mom divorced him. To support my four-year-old brother and me, my mom — leaving us entirely on our own — moved to Italy when I was sixteen to work as a caregiver. For the next five years, she would send us $400 every three months for our bills, food, clothes, and other living expenses. Because my brother frequently got strep throat and high fever, I used much of our $400 to buy his antibiotics and learned to administer shots.

We were two kids alone for five years in a tiny apartment, afraid because the bill collectors were banging at our door to cut off yet another utility and demand payment, leaving us many times with no gas or heat in 10°F winters.

During this period, I learned the crucial lesson of managing money wisely as a 16-year-old solely responsible for raising my four-year-old brother on a mere $133 a month.

At age 21, I stayed in the USA with only $20, a bag of clothes, no English, no acquaintances, and desperate to reach the American dream. Ironically I knew six languages but English was not one of them. I had no backup plan; I was financially illiterate, insecure, naïve, and clueless about how I would make it. I slept on the bare floor, covering myself with the one sheet I brought. Eight weeks after staying, I was struggling to adapt with insecurities creeping up, on the verge of giving up, and even called an airline to book a flight back to Moldova.

As I was packing and tears streamed down my face, I found the strength to pull myself together. I told myself, *This is not who you are. The only way you are a failure is if you give up. You can't stop when things get difficult. You have been through the worst. You have to push through to build a future where your kids never find themselves orphans because you didn't have the education and money to support them.*

Oh boy, it was a journey! I worked as a restaurant waitress and lived with people to make ends meet. I failed at so many things, including my first business.

As Thomas A. Edison once said, "I have not failed. I've just found 10,000 ways that won't work."

But I chose to learn from books and courses, seeking mentors and hiring coaches to speed up my success by learning from their mistakes and achievements. Also, I joined groups of wealthy people to build relationships and life-long friendships. All of which contributed to me eventually building a stock market portfolio and investing in real estate.

I am thrilled to have you here with me, embarking on a transformative journey toward a more prosperous life. If you're reading this, it means that you've made a conscious choice to take control of your financial destiny and start creating the life you've always dreamed of. I am here to be your companion and guide on this exciting adventure.

Before we dive into the nitty-gritty of mastering the art of a prosperous life, in the first paragraph, I opened the door to one of the most impactful moments in my life that sparked my passion for this topic. My financial and prosperous life journey wasn't always smooth sailing. In fact, it was filled with obstacles, heartaches, and lessons learned the hard way. But through it all, I discovered a powerful truth: the power of choice.

That moment was when I realized that life is all about choice: my stepfather's choice to end or sustain my mother's life, let my difficult childhood hold me back, or use it as a building block to something better. My choices since then have led me to where I am today — a successful corporate career that I left behind, an entrepreneur, author, wife, and proud mother of three beautiful children.

And now, I want to share the lessons I've learned and the strategies I've developed along the way with you, my friend. I want to help you unlock the secret roadmap and teach you the power of choice to lead you to a life of prosperity and fulfillment.

Throughout this book, we'll explore the following three phases, each with its sections and chapters that will provide you with the tools, knowledge, and insights you need to master the art of a prosperous life:

1. **Building a Wealth Foundation:** We'll start by examining your current wealth identity, discovering your unstoppable "why," and learning the secrets to building winning habits that will set the stage for your financial confidence.

2. **Mastering Money Management:** In this phase, we'll dive into the practical side of personal finance, exploring value-based spending, super savings plans, and learn how to get paid what you are worth, which will help you take control of your money and make it work for you.

3. **Achieving Exponential Growth:** Finally, we'll delve into the world of investing, how to calculate your Dream Life number, learn stock market investments, and unlock the power of real estate passive income.

As we journey together, I'll be sharing with you my own experiences, challenges, and triumphs, as well as those of others who have successfully navigated their way to financial confidence to pave their way to their own freedom & prosperity. We'll also discuss practical exercises and action steps you can implement immediately to start seeing results in your own life.

Now, you might wonder, *Why should I trust you, of all people, to guide me on this journey?* And that's a valid question. After all, there are countless financial gurus, experts, and self-proclaimed "money mentors" out there, each with their take on what it takes to achieve financial success.

But here's the thing: I'm not just another "expert" spouting advice. I've been in your shoes — someone who's struggled, stumbled, and picked myself back up again to continue creating a life of true fulfillment. I've learned through trial and error, and I've developed a system that has worked for others who have followed in my footsteps.

This book isn't just about theory — it's about real-world, practical strategies that have been proven to work. And it is not only about financial success — I'm talking about the success that impacts every area of your life, from your relationships to your career to your personal well-being.

One of the most important things I've learned on my journey is that financial prosperity is about so much more than just making money. It's about making choices that empower you to live a life of purpose, passion, and fulfillment. It's about investing in yourself and the people you love and creating a legacy that will continue to impact the world long after you're gone.

This book is your roadmap to understanding the power of choice and mastering your prosperous life. You'll find stories of people from various walks of life who have made the conscious decision to build their lives according to their values and beliefs.

For me, a prosperous life means putting God first, being a loving wife, a present mother for my children, and being the best version of myself for everyone around me. I believe that rooting everything we do in God is the key to building unshakable wealth.

Throughout this book, we'll explore the idea of choice and the impact our decisions have on our financial future. We'll look at how to make better choices, break free from the limiting beliefs that hold us back, and harness the power of our mind to manifest the life we truly desire.

This journey is about more than just money — it's about discovering your purpose, unlocking your potential, and living a truly rich life in every sense of the word.

So, my dear friend, are you ready to embark on this exciting adventure? Are you ready to make the choices that will lead you to a life of financial confidence, personal fulfillment, unshakable wealth, and a prosperous future?

I believe in you and know that, together, we can create a truly extraordinary life.

As we proceed through this book, I encourage you to approach each chapter with an open mind and heart. I invite you to challenge your current beliefs about money, success, and happiness and embrace the possibilities that await you when you choose to live a life of abundance.

And remember, my friend, the journey to financial prosperity is not a sprint — it's a marathon. It takes time, patience, and persistence, but I promise you that with each step forward, you'll gain confidence, clarity, and the knowledge to get you closer to creating a life that is truly worth living.

With love and gratitude,

Your down-to-earth friend and guide on this journey to a prosperous life.

"The path to financial freedom is paved with purposeful choices, unwavering commitment, and the wisdom to manage your money with intention; for when we master our finances, we unlock the doors to our dreams." - Larisa Olteanu

PHASE 1

Building a Wealth Foundation

"Wealth isn't something that just happens. It's something you create through intentional choices and actions."- Larisa Olteanu

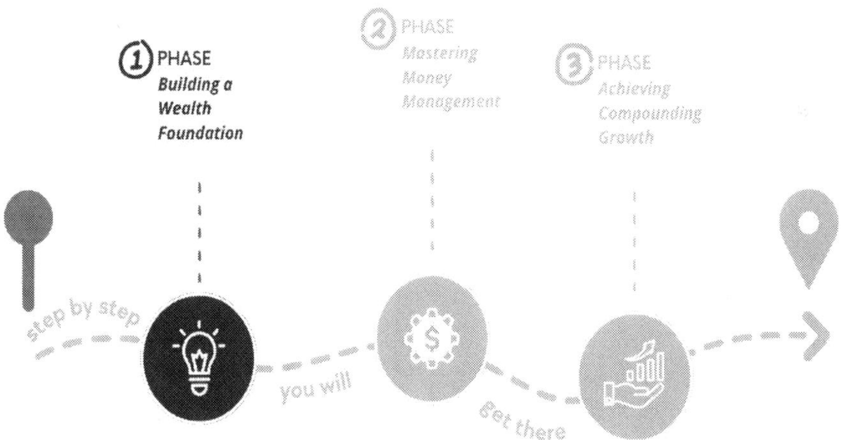

CHAPTER 1

The Unshakable Wealth Identity

1.1 - Establish Your New Wealth Identity

"You don't attract what you want. You attract what you are." - Dr. Wayne Dyer

Have you ever wondered why a tiny fraction of this world's population holds most of the wealth? It's because the top 1% are anchored in their wealth identity, which influences their thoughts, feelings, and actions. This is what sets them apart from others who might crave riches but lack the mindset to truly achieve them.

You might think, *But I don't believe my thoughts and attitudes affect my finances*, or *I don't want to change who I am just to become wealthy.* I understand your concerns, but the reality is that to achieve true financial success, it's vital to address the limiting beliefs and negative thought patterns that may be holding you back.

To truly break free from your financial rut, you must address the pain points stemming from your current mindset. Feeling stuck in a cycle of limited opportunities and struggling to achieve your financial goals despite your hard work are all signs that it's time for a change.

Your identity is linked to your self-worth; whatever your self-worth is today is your life because your self-worth is your ceiling. You will never rise above your self-worth. The money you make, the wealth you build, and the prosperous life you want will never be more than what you believe you are worthy of in your current identity. Every area of your life will meet you at the level of your self-worth.

Cultivating a new wealth identity involves recognizing the power of your beliefs and attitudes and how they impact your financial success. As you develop this new identity, you'll become more aware of the limiting beliefs that have held you back, and you'll be equipped to replace them with empowering beliefs that will drive you toward financial freedom.

Embracing a new wealth identity allows you to realign your mindset with your goals, become more resilient in the face of challenges, and find fulfillment and purpose in your financial journey. This transformation will also unlock your full potential, accelerating your growth and enabling you to positively impact others and leave a lasting legacy.

My journey to discovering the secrets of true wealth-building began with understanding my worth, my identity in Christ, and God's plan for an abundant life. But before we dive in, let's see some of the differences between a wealthy mindset and a broke mindset.

Broke people often derive their identity from their material possessions, such as houses, cars, clothes, and money. On the other hand, wealthy people root their identity in who they are, not what they own. They understand that money expresses their true selves, so they remain confident and content with their well-being.

Moreover, broke people work for money, while wealthy people's money works hard for them. The former either spend their days living in fear of losing money, so they miss great opportunities or spend it on themselves, whereas the latter dream of their legacy and know how to make their money work for them. This wisdom and power to create wealth give wealthy people confidence and the courage to face the future.

Most people don't consider identity change when they embark on a journey of self-improvement. They think, *I want to be rich* (outcome), *and if I stick to this budget, then I'll be rich* (process).

But the thing is, our thoughts about ourselves range from positive to negative, and when these thoughts come together, they create our personal identity. This identity, in turn, shapes our beliefs, which drive our behavior. If your identity aligns with your goals, you can take the actions needed to achieve them.

So, at the core of living a prosperous life lies the art of mastering your own identity. To achieve true financial confidence and lasting abundance, it's essential to cultivate a wealth identity that shapes your thoughts, emotions, and actions. This transformative journey requires a deep understanding of the fundamental principles that contribute to lasting success and happiness.

But why is building a new identity so crucial to mastering the art of living a prosperous life? The answer lies in the power of our beliefs and the subconscious patterns that drive our behavior. Our identity is the sum of these beliefs and patterns, which determine how we perceive the world, react to challenges, and, ultimately, how successful we become.

When we begin our journey towards prosperity, we often carry with us limiting beliefs and negative thought patterns ingrained from our upbringing, society, or past experiences. These mental roadblocks can prevent us from realizing our full potential and achieving our desired abundant life. We must delve deep within ourselves to overcome these obstacles, identify the limiting factors, and consciously reshape our identity. Creating a new wealth identity is an empowering process that enables you to:

1. **Realign your mindset with your goals.**

   A strong and unshakable wealth identity aligns your mindset with your financial goals. As you embrace this new identity, you'll develop empowering beliefs and thought patterns that facilitate success. This alignment propels you to take consistent and focused action, leading to a prosperous life.

2. **Embrace resilience in challenging times.**

   Building a new wealth identity requires resilience and adaptability. Life has setbacks and challenges, but a prosperous mindset enables you to navigate these obstacles with grace and determination. By adopting an identity rooted in abundance, you'll cultivate the mental strength to persevere through difficult times and emerge even stronger.

3. **Discover purpose and fulfillment.**

   A prosperous life isn't solely about financial success; it's also about living purposefully and experiencing genuine fulfillment. As you develop a new wealth identity, you'll gain clarity on your values, passions, and goals, allowing you to live a life connected to your true self. This sense of purpose fuels your motivation and enhances your overall well-being and happiness.

4. **Unlock your full potential and accelerate your growth.**

   Embracing a new wealth identity opens the door to personal growth and self-discovery. As you challenge your limiting beliefs and explore new possibilities, you'll unlock your full potential and accelerate your growth. This ongoing process of self-improvement is an integral aspect of living a prosperous life and achieving lasting success.

5. **Create a positive impact on others and leave a lasting legacy.**

   A wealth identity grounded in abundance and prosperity gives you the ability to make a meaningful impact on the lives of others. Your success, driven by your newfound identity, will inspire and empower those around you to live life to the fullest while pursuing their dreams. By cultivating a wealth identity, you are building a brighter future for yourself and creating a lasting impact for future generations.

Now that we understand the transformative power of building a new wealth identity, how do we make the shift? How do we create a new wealth identity that will change our lives? Let's explore the practical steps you can take to make this shift in your life:

1. **Decide who you want to be as a person.**

   We all possess enormous potential, but many crumble under pressure or never even try. When you know who you want to be, you can confidently and boldly achieve your dreams. Visualize the best version of yourself daily and ask yourself in every situation what would a person with a prosperous life do. How would an abundant person act in a difficult situation, in traffic, or at a restaurant? What are the character traits of a prosperous, abundant person I can model to become one? What would be the best version of myself that I would be proud of? What would an awesome, patient, and loving person do in this difficult situation? And start handling and living life as such.

   Set aside some time to introspect and identify the qualities you believe are essential for a wealthy, abundant, and prosperous identity. For instance, you may choose to be disciplined, resourceful, generous, and open-minded. Reflect on these qualities and write them down to remind yourself of the person you're striving to become.

2. **Choose your company wisely.**

You know what they say, "Show me your friends, and I'll tell you who you are." It might sound cliché, but it couldn't be more accurate. The company you keep has a huge impact on your life, and if you aim to join the ranks of the affluent, it's time to level up your network, my friend.

First, take a hard and honest look at the people you surround yourself with. Are they lifting you up or weighing you down? Are they empowering you to reach for the stars or pouring their fears and failures onto you? Surrounding yourself with people who share your ambition and drive is essential. And I know it's not always easy, but sometimes we have to bid farewell to the naysayers and "Debbie Downers" that hold us back.

One way to kick-start your journey to wealth is by joining communities of people who share your financial goals. But let's not stop there. Seek out mentors who are where you want to be one, five, or even ten years from now. These people have already walked the path, made mistakes, and can provide valuable insights to help you avoid those pesky pitfalls. Why swim in muddy waters when you can learn from the best and fast-track your way to success? Choose your mentors wisely and let them be your guiding stars as you embark on this incredible journey towards financial confidence & prosperity.

At the same time, add value to the people around you, including your mentors. See what you can help them with and be there for them when they need you. Relationships are not a one-way street. Life is about helping and serving others; the more you serve, the more fulfilling and prosperous your life becomes. Just remember the last time you were able to help someone, and it changed their life. I bet it was a deep and joyful experience you will cherish forever. God calls us to love others, so love everyone around you and truly get to know who they are and the greatness in them.

3. **Embrace a growth mindset.**

A growth mindset is the understanding that one's intelligence, skills, and talents are not fixed but can be enhanced and expanded through commitment, resilience, and continued learning. Don't give up when you hit setbacks, embrace challenges, and view failure as an opportunity for growth. This mindset will help you stay open to new possibilities and experiences that can accelerate your journey toward building an abundant identity.

Andrew Carnegie is a famous example of someone who established a new wealth identity and succeeded in both life and finances. Born in Scotland in 1835, Carnegie grew up in poverty, with his family immigrating to the United States when he was a teenager. Despite his humble beginnings, Carnegie established himself as one of the wealthiest and most influential businesspeople in American history. He effectively transformed his identity from a poor immigrant to a capable and ambitious individual.

Carnegie's transformation began with his mindset. He was an avid reader and learner, believing in the power of self-improvement and education. He borrowed books from a local benefactor, Colonel James Anderson, whose generosity inspired Carnegie's lifelong commitment to philanthropy and the establishment of public libraries.

As Carnegie's knowledge and skills grew, so did his ambition. He worked various jobs, eventually landing a position as a telegraph operator to Thomas A. Scott, a superintendent at the Pennsylvania Railroad Company. This connection would prove vital in Carnegie's rise to wealth, as he learned valuable lessons about business and investment from Scott.

Carnegie's newfound wealth identity fueled his drive for success. He invested strategically in growing industries, such as iron and steel, and leveraged his connections and business acumen to build an empire. By the late 1800s, his company, Carnegie Steel, was the world's largest and most profitable steel company.

In 1901, Carnegie sold his steel company to J.P. Morgan for a staggering $480 million[1] (over $14 billion today), cementing his status as one of the wealthiest people in history. Carnegie then turned his attention to philanthropy, donating millions of dollars to establish libraries, schools, and universities and funding scientific research and world peace initiatives.

Andrew Carnegie's journey from poverty to immense wealth and philanthropy exemplifies the power of establishing a new wealth identity. Through a commitment to self-improvement, strategic decision-making, building and leveraging his network, and a focus on creating value, Carnegie transformed his life and left a lasting impact on the world.

Wealth-building is more driven by behaviors than math. Making sound financial decisions largely hinges on managing your emotions, expectations, and behaviors. Understanding your own psychology and biases can help you make better financial choices.

The ability to adapt during challenging times is crucial for financial success. Emphasize adaptability and learn from your financial and life mistakes.

---

[1] https://www.carnegie.org/interactives/foundersstory/#!/

Very few people talk about emotional intelligence's key role in making sound financial decisions. Managing emotions, practicing self-awareness, and maintaining discipline can lead to better financial outcomes.

4. **Adopt a long-term perspective when it comes to personal finance.**

This will help you weather short-term setbacks and stay focused on your financial goals.

Remember, the journey to true financial success is not about accumulating material possessions but rather about developing a wealth identity rooted in self-awareness, purpose, and long-term thinking. By following these steps and nurturing your wealth identity, you are much closer to joining the thriving and abundant path.

As you continue on this journey, celebrate your progress, and cherish the small victories. With each step, you become the person you need to be to achieve true financial independence. The path forward might not be a smooth ride, but with determination, support, and the right mindset, you will undoubtedly transform your life and start mastering the unshakable identity you need.

In the words of the wise King Solomon, "A good person leaves an inheritance for their children's children" (Proverbs 13:22). By cultivating your wealth identity, you are building a brighter future for yourself and creating a lasting impact for generations to come.

With the right mindset and unwavering commitment, the world is truly your oyster. Here's to the unshakable wealth identity that will carry you to the heights of financial success and beyond!

By following these principles and going chapter by chapter in this book while taking consistent actions, you'll continue building a strong wealth identity and create a fulfilling, purpose-driven, and abundant life. Financial success is about more than just money — it's about embracing a mindset that allows you to live life on your terms and leave a lasting legacy.

Very Next Action Steps

1. **Define your ideal wealth identity:** Reflect on the qualities and characteristics of a prosperous, abundant, and wealthy person. Write these qualities down and visualize yourself embodying them in various situations. Consider the best version of yourself and align your thoughts, emotions, and actions with this new identity.

2. **Surround yourself with a supportive network:** Evaluate the company you keep and ensure they are uplifting and empowering rather than holding you back. Join communities with similar financial goals and seek out mentors who have achieved what you desire. Take their experiences, learn from them, and apply insights to your own journey.

3. **Cultivate a growth mindset:** Embrace challenges, learn from setbacks, and view failures as opportunities for growth. Develop emotional intelligence and maintain discipline to make better financial decisions. Focus on long-term goals, adapt to changing circumstances, and learn from financial and life mistakes.

1.2 - Discover Your Unstoppable "Why"

"Rooted in your 'Why,' you become an unshakable mountain, weathering life's storms and rising above to embrace a life of true prosperity, wealth, and abundance."

Your "why" is the unstoppable force that propels you toward your dreams, and nothing can hold you back! Too many people struggle to build wealth, achieve financial freedom, and truly savor an abundant life because they haven't found their "Why." They might feel unfulfilled, uncertain about the future, or need direction and purpose in their financial goals. However, when you're anchored in your genuine "Why," you become an unshakable mountain standing tall against stormy ocean waves. You remain steadfast no matter how hard life's waves of hardships crash against you.

I heard many people say, "I don't need a reason to want to be wealthy," or "I don't know what I want in the future," but the truth is, understanding your "why" is essential in maintaining motivation and focusing on your goals. While discipline is important, motivation fueled by a profound sense of purpose can lead to a more satisfying and meaningful life.

Janine Shepherd[2] was an Australian cross-country skier who aspired to compete in the Olympics. However, during a training bike ride, she was hit by a truck, resulting in severe spinal cord injuries and multiple fractures. Doctors said she would never walk again, and her dreams of becoming an Olympian seemed shattered.

Despite her physical limitations, Janine discovered her unstoppable "why": to overcome her circumstances and inspire others with her story of resilience and determination. She decided that her accident would not define her life and was committed to redefining her goals and pursuing new dreams.

---

[2] https://janineshepherd.com/about-janine/

Through sheer willpower and perseverance, Janine taught herself to walk again and became an accomplished pilot and aerobatics instructor. She went on to compete in paragliding and authored several books, sharing her story to motivate and inspire others facing adversity.

Janine's unstoppable "why" allowed her to create a new identity and achieve success through her career as a pilot, author, and motivational speaker. Her ability to adapt and find a new purpose in life has inspired many and is a testament to the power of discovering one's unstoppable "why."

Understanding the importance of "why" is essential when mastering the art of prosperous, abundant, and wealthy living. When you have a clear sense of purpose and direction in life, you can make better choices that follow your values and priorities, leading to a more satisfying and meaningful life.

Without a strong "why," you will have a hard time staying motivated and focused on your goals, especially during challenging times. But when you're driven by a purpose greater than yourself, you're more likely to push through setbacks and overcome obstacles on your way to success. Embracing your "why" also helps you stay true to yourself and your core beliefs, attracting like-minded people and fostering deeper connections, both essential for personal growth and happiness.

When your actions are fueled by a clear "why," not only do you inspire and motivate others to join you on your mission, but you also create a sense of community and belonging, which is crucial for a prosperous and abundant life. Focusing on your "why" encourages you to think beyond short-term wins and instant gratification, leading to long-term success and wealth. Moreover, it allows you to consider the impact of your actions on others and the world around you, ultimately creating a positive legacy that extends beyond material wealth and contributes to the greater good.

So, how do you start finding your unstoppable "why"? Begin by taking some time to reflect on your values, passions, and goals. What truly matters to you? What drives you to get up every morning? Next, consider the challenges and pain points in your life. What obstacles have you overcome, and what lessons have you learned? By exploring these questions and delving deep into your own experiences, you'll uncover the powerful "why" within.

Remember, your "why" is a deeply personal and unique force that propels you toward the life you dream of living. Discovering and embracing it will unlock the true potential for lasting abundance, prosperity, and wealth.

As you continue your journey toward discovering your unstoppable "why," it's crucial to cultivate a growth mindset and a willingness to learn from your experiences. Embrace your curiosity and never stop asking questions because every answer brings you one step closer to uncovering your true purpose. Build a circle of people around you who encourage and support your growth — those who inspire you to be better and help you realize the power of your "why."

One valuable exercise to help you uncover your "why" is journaling. Writing down your thoughts, feelings, and experiences can provide clarity and help you identify patterns in your life. Over time, you'll be able to connect the dots and gain a deeper understanding of your true purpose. Remember that your "why" may evolve as you grow and change, so revisit it regularly to ensure it still resonates with who you are and where you're headed.

As you become more attuned to your "why," you'll find that your approach to building wealth and abundance shifts. Instead of focusing solely on accumulating material possessions, you'll start to prioritize personal growth, relationships, and positively impacting the world. This mindset shift is crucial for creating a life of true prosperity and lasting happiness.

My students embark on a transformative journey toward uncovering their unstoppable "why" and unlocking their prosperous hero within. Through carefully crafted exercises and guided reflections, participants delve deep into their core beliefs, values, and passions to reveal the driving force behind their desire for wealth and abundance.

One powerful and transformative exercise in the program is finding your deep "why" exercise. This exercise encourages students to dig deep within themselves, peeling back the layers of their motivations and desires until they reach the heart of their "why." Each level explores a different aspect of purpose, with every subsequent layer revealing a more profound and meaningful understanding of what truly drives them. As students work through this exercise, they often experience profound moments of clarity, self-discovery, and personal growth. As Dean Graziosi wisely said, "You don't know your 'why' until you cry."

As the prosperous hero awakens within them, students begin to see a noticeable shift in their mindset and approach to life. No longer held back by limiting beliefs and negative thought patterns, they become an unstoppable force, daring not only to dream but to act and turn their dreams into reality. This powerful transformation enables them to tackle challenges head-on, persevere in adversity, and stay committed to their goals, ultimately leading to a life of true wealth and prosperity.

By discovering their unstoppable "why," students unlock their full potential and learn to harness the power of their prosperous hero within. This newfound clarity, motivation, and resilience propel them towards a life of abundance, happiness, and purpose, where they get closer to achieving their financial goals and making a meaningful impact on the world around them.

Very Next Action Steps

1. **Reflect on your values, passions, and goals:** Set aside some quiet time to ponder what truly matters to you, what drives you to get up every morning, and what you genuinely care about. This introspection will help you identify the core aspects of your life that resonate with your inner being and may eventually lead you to your "why."

2. **Journal your thoughts, feelings, and experiences:** Start a daily journaling practice to gain clarity and insight into your life. Write down your thoughts, feelings, and experiences; over time, you'll see patterns and connections that reveal your true purpose. Remember to revisit your "why" regularly, as it may evolve as you grow and change.

1.3 - Secrets to Building Winning Habits

"We are what we repeatedly do. Excellence, then, is not an act, but a habit."
- Aristotle

It was a rainy evening in Houston, Texas, and I found myself locked away in my tiny room, pouring over textbooks and scribbling notes. I longed for my family, which was miles away, and prayed for things to work as I prepared for the recruiting season, where I hoped to lock in a dream job. I knew that if I wanted a better life for myself and my family, I had to rise above my circumstances, make conscious & intentional choices that aligned with my goals, and overcome the habits that held me back.

In that dimly lit room, I realized the importance of cultivating winning habits, and from then on, I committed to breaking free from the chains of mediocrity. It's been quite a journey, and today, I'm here to share with you the secrets to building winning habits that have helped me and countless others create a life of success.

Our lives are often filled with stress, distractions, and competing priorities, making staying focused on our financial goals challenging. We all have bad habits; some are obvious, some are hidden, and they keep us from achieving our full potential. You may find yourself impulse-buying, procrastinating on saving or neglecting your investments. These bad habits can be difficult to break, especially when you're overwhelmed or feel like your financial goals are out of reach. You might even find yourself thinking, *I don't need habits to be successful. I've tried to form new habits before and failed*, or *I don't have the time or energy to form new habits.* But by understanding their underlying causes and developing a plan to replace them with positive behaviors, you can overcome these obstacles and set yourself on the path to financial success. This section will reveal the secrets to building winning habits and how to incorporate them into your daily routine.

Before we dive into the winning habits, let's take a moment to discuss why habits are so crucial in building an abundant life. Our habits shape our lives and are responsible for our successes and failures. As Aristotle once said, "We are what we repeatedly do. Excellence, then, is not an act, but a habit." By identifying the habits holding you back and replacing them with winning habits, you can create a solid foundation for a prosperous and abundant life.

You might be wondering how small changes in your daily routine can have such a transformative impact on your life, but the truth is, its seemingly insignificant actions compound over time to create lasting change. Just as a single drop of water can carve a path through solid rock, the consistent practice of small, positive habits can shape the course of your financial future.

To truly grasp the power of winning habits, consider the story of two friends, John and Sarah. They had similar backgrounds and jobs but vastly different financial habits. John lived paycheck to paycheck, never bothering to save money or invest in his future. Sarah, meanwhile, diligently saved a small percentage of her income each month and consistently invested in her financial education.

Over time, these seemingly minor differences in their daily habits led to dramatically different financial outcomes. John continued to struggle, always feeling like he was treading water financially. Sarah, however, built a stable foundation of wealth and abundance that allowed her to enjoy a life of financial freedom and security.

What set Sarah apart from John was her commitment to winning habits. By consistently practicing small, manageable actions, she created a powerful momentum that propelled her toward her wealth goals. Like a snowball gaining momentum when rolling down a hill, this momentum grew larger and more unstoppable with each passing day.

You, too, can harness the power of winning habits to create a life of abundance and prosperity.

Let's dive into the first part of our journey: identifying and overcoming the habits that hold you back from living your dream life. Remember, my friend, awareness is the first step toward change.

One of the most common habits that hold people back is procrastination. We've all been there, putting off important tasks, only to find ourselves buried under a mountain of to-dos. Procrastination isn't just an inconvenience; it's a dream killer. To build winning habits, you must recognize when you're delaying crucial tasks and commit to taking immediate action. Break down your goals into more manageable steps and tackle them one at a time. Creating goals is mastery, and we will cover it later in this book. Before you know it, you'll be making meaningful progress toward your dreams.

Furthermore, the inability to prioritize tasks can significantly impede your progress toward success. It's easy to get trapped in the whirlwind of daily life, attending to every little thing that comes your way. However, not all tasks are created equal. To build winning habits, you need to identify the tasks that genuinely matter, bring you closer to your goals, and focus your energy on them. Delegate or eliminate the rest and watch as your productivity soars.

Lastly, the fear of failure is a significant roadblock to success. This fear can be paralyzing, preventing you from taking risks and exploring beyond your comfort zone. It's essential to understand that failure is a natural part of the learning process. Embrace, learn from, and use it as a stepping stone toward your goals. Don't let the fear of failure keep you from pursuing the life you've always dreamt of.

In my journey toward financial freedom, I've encountered countless obstacles, setbacks, and frustrations. But through persistence and determination, I've discovered the secret to building winning habits that has transformed not only my financial life but every aspect of my existence. Now, I want to share this powerful secret with you so you can enjoy a life of abundance and prosperity.

Imagine waking up each day with a clear vision of your financial goals, knowing you're consistently taking small but powerful steps toward achieving them. Picture yourself confidently navigating the world of personal finance, making informed decisions, and watching your wealth grow over time. This is the power of winning habits — I'm here to show you how to create them.

The secret of building winning habits is anchored in the framework of mastering the habit loops one tiny habit at a time and stacking those habits for maximum success.

The habit loop has three components: a cue, a routine, and a reward. Understanding and manipulating these habit loops can help you form new, positive habits or replace negative ones. This is how these elements work:

- **Cue:** The cue is the trigger that initiates the habit loop. The trigger can be a particular time, place, emotional condition, circumstance, or any other environmental factor that prompts the behavior. For example, a notification that your paycheck was deposited is a cue to go shopping.

- **Routine:** The routine is the actual behavior or habit that responds to the cue. In our example, the routine would be driving to the store or online shopping every time your paycheck notification goes off.

- **Reward:** The reward is the positive reinforcement or benefit from completing the routine. The reward helps solidify the habit and motivates you to repeat the routine in the future. In our example, the reward might be making the purchase or waiting for the package to arrive and getting a momentary "feel good" experience due to the release of dopamine — a hormone that lights up our brain and fuels excitement.

To apply the habit loop principles, start by analyzing your existing habits and identifying the cues, routines, and rewards associated with positive and negative behaviors. Then, replace negative routines with positive ones that satisfy the same rewards, and reinforce these new habits by being mindful of the rewards and consistently practicing the routines in response to their cues.

Note: It's best to start focusing on creating small, easily achievable habits that can lead to more significant behavioral changes over time. Small habits can be more effective in creating lasting change than attempting to make drastic lifestyle adjustments.

Once you have identified the cues, routines, and rewards associated with a specific behavior, choose a small, manageable action that aligns with your larger goal. For example, if your goal is financial success, you could start by setting aside 1% of your monthly income. And, to anchor the new habit, link the new behavior to an existing routine or habit. This connection helps ensure the new habit becomes integral to your daily life. For example, you could set aside money each time you receive a paycheck.

Continue analyzing your existing financial habits and identifying areas where improvement is needed. For example, consider your daily spending patterns. Do you find yourself impulsively buying? Or are you prone to online shopping sprees when you're feeling stressed? These seemingly small behaviors can quickly add up, draining your bank account and sabotaging your wealth-building efforts.

Now, think about how you can replace these negative habits with more positive, empowering actions. When you feel the urge to shop online, redirect that energy towards a healthier outlet, like going for a walk or meditating. You'll gradually shift your behaviors and progress toward your financial goals by consistently practicing these small changes.

As you work on incorporating winning habits into your daily routine, remember the importance of anchoring these new behaviors to existing habits by stacking them. This will help you stay consistent and ensure that your winning habits become integral to your life. For example, you could anchor your new savings habit to your morning coffee ritual. Each time you pack your lunch at home to take to work, transfer the money you would have spent on a restaurant lunch salad to your savings account. Over time, this small action will accumulate into a substantial nest egg.

How do you anchor these habits into existing routines? Combining several small habits into a cohesive routine allows you to efficiently work towards your financial goals while minimizing the time and effort required. For instance, create a daily or weekly financial routine that includes reviewing expenses, updating your spending plan, and setting short-term financial goals. This streamlined approach helps you stay focused and ensures that you're consistently making progress toward your wealth and abundance objectives.

Our brains are wired to seek positive reinforcement, so when you celebrate your achievements, you strengthen the neural pathways associated with your new habits, making them more likely to stick. Set up a system of reminders to help you stay on track with your financial habit stack. This could include setting alarms on your phone, placing visual cues around your home, or even getting the support of a friend or family member to hold you accountable.

Celebrating your successes and wins, even those that may seem small, is important. Therefore, each time you complete a habit from your financial routine, take a moment to acknowledge your accomplishment. This positive reinforcement will help solidify your new habits and make them feel more enjoyable and rewarding.

Finally, be prepared to adapt and adjust your habits as needed. Life is constantly changing, and what works for you now might not be the best approach in the future. Regularly evaluate your financial habits and make any necessary adjustments to ensure they continue to support your wealth and abundance goals. For example, you might find your initial investing goal too easy, and you're ready to challenge yourself by increasing the amount you set aside each month.

By consistently practicing these winning habits and integrating them into your daily life, you'll begin to see a transformation in your financial situation. Your relationship with money will improve, and you'll find yourself making more informed decisions, feeling more in control, and ultimately moving closer to your wealth and abundance goals.

Note: To master the art of a prosperous life, you must develop winning habits with the above framework for *every* area of your life, spiritual, mental, physical, and emotional health, as well as relationship and career or business success.

In summary, the secret to building winning habits lies in understanding the mechanics of habit formation. By analyzing your existing financial habits, selecting small, manageable actions, creating habit loops, anchoring new behaviors to existing routines, combining habits into a habit stack, setting triggers and reminders, celebrating success, and adapting as needed, you'll be closer to achieving your wealth and abundance dreams. Embrace the power of these winning habits and watch your financial life transform, one small step at a time.

Don't take my word for it...

"I was blown away by how valuable all of the information I learned from Lari has been and how much it has changed my life. I have not only been able to pay off $15,000 of debt, but also start an emergency fund and have saved $8,000, but also negotiate a $20,000 dollar salary increase with my current employer!! And have a clear and structured plan for building my own business!"

- Bogdan C.

Very Next Action Steps

1. **Identify and replace negative habits:** Reflect on your current financial habits and pinpoint those that hinder your progress toward your goals. Replace these negative habits with positive ones that align with your financial objectives. For instance, if you tend to impulsively shop online, redirect that urge towards healthier activities like walking or meditating.

2. **Create a financial habit stack:** Combine several small, positive habits into a cohesive routine to make incorporating them into your daily life easier. For example, develop a daily or weekly financial routine that includes reviewing expenses, updating your spending plan, and setting short-term financial goals. Consistently practice this habit stack to create lasting change.

3. **Set triggers and reminders, and celebrate small wins:** Establish a system of reminders to help you stay on track with your new financial habits. Set alarms on your phone, use visual cues around your home or enlist the support of a friend or family member for accountability. Remember to celebrate big and small achievements, as positive reinforcement strengthens your commitment to your new habits and makes them more likely to stick.

CHAPTER 2

Conquering Your Dreams

2.1 - Shatter Limiting Beliefs and Dream Big

"What we think, we become." - Mahatma Gandhi

My knees were shaking, my skin was turning pale, and my whole body was experiencing a wave of stress electricity as I was hiding behind the desk, as much as I could, while vigorously praying and trying to appear posed, calm, and ready. I was about to be called to my death sentence in front of the whole class by a math teacher who pulled your soul out just by looking at you. That day my prayer didn't work — "Larisa to the board to solve these polynomials." I had no idea what this alien word meant, and how in the world was I going to solve any of that gibberish writing called "math" on the board? As I stood in front of the board, not knowing what to do, with my head down, completely embarrassed to look at my classmates, and fearing I would be mocked or laughed at, one thought kept running through my head: *You are clueless in math, you are so weak, such a loser.*

See, throughout my childhood, there was a story I had built in my head that was true to me, but it wasn't me. It was built by the people around me and my life experiences. One of those experiences happened three years before this embarrassing day when I was called to the board. I was diagnosed with a severe case of pneumonia which kept me away from school for three months. I missed all that material, and since my parents couldn't afford to pay for tutoring to bring me up to speed, I went back to school with an educational gap that turned into a monster by the time I got to the 5th grade.

For three years, I struggled, and kids around me, being kids, laughed and called me names that built in my subconscious a story and a set of limiting beliefs around not being good in school, unintelligent, weak, and an unconfident person. Until this one day in the 6th grade, when I made the conscious choice, out of nowhere, to start telling myself, *I know math, I am great at math, I love math,* and *math comes easy to me.* Without realizing it, this was the first time I squashed limiting beliefs about my abilities and changed them into empowering beliefs. Sure enough, my math grades went up, and as funny as it sounds, math became my favorite subject.

Yet, it wasn't until decades later that I realized how many limiting beliefs we have around money and how destructive the stories we carry throughout our lives are to our dreams and the prosperous life we are destined to live. How many times have you stopped to question your beliefs? Where do they come from? Are they true? Or do you believe them because that's what you have always known to be your world? These beliefs might be true to you, but not truly you!

Years after I stayed in the U.S., I had just finished reading *The Science of Getting Rich* by Wallace D. Wattles, and it was like a light bulb went off in my head. Suddenly, I shifted my mindset about money and everything that came with it. How I looked at work, life, and even success began to transform.

Before this change, I used to say I didn't want to be rich. I thought having a lot of money would bring stress to my life, and I didn't need that. But as I was reading that book, something clicked inside me. I realized that my understanding of money was flawed, holding me back from living the life I truly wanted.

It took some time for me to fully embrace this shift, but I'm so grateful I did. Now, I'm on a mission to help others break free from their limiting beliefs about money and find the success they deserve. And that's where this journey begins - examining our beliefs about money and making the necessary changes to empower ourselves.

It's important to recognize the problems you face, like struggling with negative thoughts and limiting beliefs that hold you back, a lack of motivation and drive to pursue goals and build wealth, and feeling unfulfilled and unsatisfied with your current life despite being blessed in many other areas, including the most valuable of all, the gift of life.

With social media, you might constantly be comparing yourself to others and feeling like you do not measure up, feeling like you're stuck and have no idea how to break free, and struggling to find purpose and meaning in your life, which can seem insurmountable. And, with the busyness of life, who has the time for self-reflection? But if you don't stop and take the time to get clarity, and focus on bringing your inner world into peace and order, then who would? And how can you bring happiness and fulfillment into your external world? The truth and the great news is you are in charge of your inner world, and the sooner you take the time to work on it, the faster you will see changes in your life.

Many people, including some of my students who start this journey, say, "I'm skeptical of the benefits of a positive mindset and don't think it will make a difference. I am practical." By "practical," they mean seeing everything doom and gloom. If you live a life you don't enjoy, filled with "practical" ways and limiting beliefs, it's painful, and you know you are in the wrong movie, so why would you continue holding on to the existing mindset patterns? Isn't it time to try something new? How would a positive mindset hurt you? What would you lose if you let go of those limiting beliefs holding you back from your greatest life? I assure you that addressing and overcoming these limiting beliefs can transform your life in incredible ways.

The thing is, only some are ready to make that leap. Some people might be comfortable with their current mindset and not open to changing it. But for people like you, who are, the transformation can be life-changing.

As I dove deeper into my money mindset, I realized there were two types of beliefs: limiting beliefs and empowering beliefs. Limiting beliefs are thoughts we have about money that stop us from reaching the best version of ourselves and our full potential. On the other hand, empowering beliefs help us to move forward and create the abundance we desire.

One of the most common limiting beliefs I found was that working harder would make me wealthy. This belief kept me in survival mode, working long hours at multiple jobs, but I never really got ahead. However, when I began to adopt empowering beliefs, I discovered that working smarter, not harder, was the key to true wealth and success.

As I shifted my mindset from limiting to empowering beliefs, I noticed how my actions and decisions started to change. Instead of being afraid to take risks or expand my business, I confidently pursued new growth opportunities.

The truth is our beliefs about money can either limit or empower us. We're stuck in a cycle of stress and scarcity when we hold onto limiting beliefs. But when we embrace empowering beliefs, we open ourselves to a world of abundance and prosperity.

Breaking free from limiting beliefs isn't always easy, but it's worth the effort. As we challenge our beliefs and replace them with empowering ones, we can begin to transform our lives in incredible ways.

One of the most effective ways to do this is by questioning our beliefs and asking ourselves if they're truly serving us. For example, is the belief that money is evil, helping or hindering our success? By examining these beliefs and replacing them with more empowering ones, we can start to create a more abundant and fulfilling life.

Once we start making these changes, we can finally step out of survival mode and focus on creating the life we truly want. This means living in a comfortable home, enjoying our work, and helping others along the way.

But remember, this transformation doesn't happen overnight. It takes time and intentional effort to shift your mindset and embrace new, empowering beliefs. However, with persistence and dedication, we can all overcome our money-limiting beliefs and create a life of abundance and prosperity.

So, are you ready to join me on this journey? Let's bust those money-limiting beliefs together and start living the life we've always dreamed of. It's time to embrace change, take control of our finances, and create a future filled with success, happiness, and abundance.

By changing our thoughts, we change our actions and, consequently, our results. The transformation that occurs when we shift our mindset and break free from limiting beliefs is powerful and can lead to incredible growth in our lives.

For example, when I first began my entrepreneurial journey, I had the mindset that I needed to work harder and harder to achieve success. This belief led me to work long hours, sacrifice my personal life, and ultimately, I became burnt out. It wasn't until I shifted my mindset and realized that working smarter, not harder, would lead me to the success I was seeking.

As you continue on the journey of turning your dreams into reality, remember that embracing a more empowering mindset will allow you to make better decisions and take actions that align with your goals. In doing so, you'll be able to create a life that is abundant, fulfilling, and in line with your true purpose.

One key element of building an abundant and successful life is understanding the concept of risk. Many people associate risk with loss or failure, but the truth is that risk is simply a part of life. In fact, taking calculated risks can lead to incredible growth and progress. The key is to manage risk effectively and make decisions based on a thorough understanding of the potential outcomes.

When you embrace the idea that risk is manageable, you can take bolder steps toward your goals without being crippled by fear or uncertainty. This mindset shift can be the catalyst for the kind of change and growth that leads to a life of abundance and success.

Another important mindset shift is recognizing that your personal and professional growth is interconnected. As you work to change your beliefs and habits around money, you'll find that this growth naturally spills over into other areas of your life. When you're open to learning and growing, you're better equipped to navigate the challenges and opportunities that come your way.

For example, as you begin to build your wealth and invest in yourself, you may find that your relationships improve, your health flourishes, and your overall sense of happiness and fulfillment increases. This holistic approach to personal growth can have a transformative impact on your life.

As you continue this journey of self-discovery and growth, it's important to surround yourself with like-minded individuals who support and uplift you. Building a community of people who share your values and aspirations can be incredibly motivating and empowering.

However, remember that not everyone will be ready to join you on this journey. It's natural for some people to resist change or to be skeptical of the ideas and beliefs that you're embracing. It's important to remember that everyone is on their own path, and it's not your responsibility to convince them of the benefits of your new mindset.

Instead, focus on leading by example and demonstrating the positive impact that these changes have had on your life. As you continue to grow and evolve, you'll inspire others to do the same. They may even pick up that book you recommended or join you in a personal development workshop.

In conclusion, busting money-limiting beliefs is much more than changing your financial thoughts. It's a deep, transformative process that requires self-reflection, growth, and an openness to new ideas and ways of living.

As you embrace this journey and make the necessary mindset shifts, you'll find yourself living a more abundant, fulfilling life that aligns with your true purpose. And ultimately, that's what it's all about — living a rich life in every sense of the word.

Remember, the path to abundance and success starts with changing the way you think. So, challenge those limiting beliefs, embrace empowering thoughts, and watch as your life starts to change in ways you never imagined possible.

Continuing our deep dive into mastering a healthy money mindset, it's time to tackle those pesky, oh-so-common limiting beliefs that keep us playing small in the financial arena. By shining a light on these beliefs, we can understand how they've been holding us back and take intentional steps to transform them into empowering, life-changing mantras. Ready for the magic to happen? Let's get to it, my friend!

Limiting belief: Money is the root of all evil.

Can we shake off this dusty, old belief? When we see money as evil, we invite guilt and fear to tag along on our financial journey. The truth? Money is a tool, and we can choose how we wield it. Focusing on all the good we can do with money makes us more motivated to earn and manage it like a boss. Think of it this way: when you're financially abundant, you can support your favorite charities, create jobs, and make your family's life a little more magical.

Limiting belief: I don't deserve to be wealthy.

Let me tell you, you are worthy of abundance, success, and all the good things in life! Believing you don't deserve wealth keeps you from recognizing the opportunities right in front of you and from the wealth you are destined for. Embrace the mantra, "I am destined and deserving of abundance and success," and watch as you become a magnet for all the opportunities that contribute to your financial growth. Next time you're at the negotiating table, confidently ask for that higher salary or take a chance on a promising investment.

Limiting belief: You must work extremely hard to make money.

This belief has us running ourselves ragged, and for what? Burnout? An unbalanced life? No, thank you! Instead, let's shift our mindset to creating wealth through smart work and seizing opportunities. This way, we'll start looking for ways to increase our income without overworking ourselves. Maybe it's time to create that passive income stream or delegate tasks to make room for high-impact projects that truly move the needle.

Limiting belief: It's selfish to want more money.

Okay, but is it really? When we think it's selfish to desire wealth, guilt creeps in, and we end up sabotaging ourselves and missing out on opportunities. Flip the script by recognizing that wanting more money allows you to create a better life for yourself, those around you and the world. With this mindset, you'll be more proactive in pursuing your financial goals. So go ahead and start that business that provides value to the world while building your wealth.

Limiting belief: I'm not good with money.

Listen up: believing you're bad with money only makes it so. It's time to replace this limiting belief with the empowering idea that you can learn and improve your financial skills. Believe in your ability to grow and watch as you become more open to learning and applying financial management principles. Take that personal finance course, chat with a financial planner, or create a spending plan that makes sense for you.

Limiting belief: Money can't buy happiness.

While it's true that money isn't everything, let's not downplay its role in our lives. This belief can make us complacent, lacking the drive to pursue our financial goals. Instead, recognize that money provides you with the freedom and resources to create a life you love. When you see money as a means to support your happiness, you'll be more motivated to create financial abundance. So go ahead, use your wealth to travel, explore your passions, and make memories with your loved ones.

Now that we've confronted these limiting beliefs, it's time to embrace our new, empowering money mindset. By making these mindset shifts, we're setting ourselves up for success, allowing us to confidently pursue our financial goals and unlock a more abundant and fulfilling life.

And the secret to turbocharging this process? It's 3D Affirmations! By incorporating this powerful technique into your daily routine, you'll supercharge your mindset transformation and create an unshakable foundation for financial success. These 3D Affirmations act as a catalyst, helping you dissolve limiting beliefs with ease and replacing them with empowering ones that attract abundance and prosperity.

What makes 3D Affirmations so effective? It's all about the unique approach that engages your mind on a deeper level. By using affirmations in the 1st, 2nd, and 3rd person, you're targeting multiple perspectives and reinforcing the positive beliefs from various angles. This multi-dimensional approach ensures that your subconscious mind fully absorbs and internalizes the empowering messages, creating lasting change. Plus, repeating these affirmations helps form new neural pathways in your brain, further solidifying your new mindset. As you consistently practice 3D Affirmations for all areas of your life, you'll begin to notice a shift in your thoughts, feelings, and actions, ultimately leading to an improved relationship with money and a more abundant life.

The journey to financial success may not always be easy, but with the right mindset, determination, and support, you can create the abundant life you've always dreamed of. So, let's say goodbye to those limiting beliefs and hello to a future filled with possibility, growth, and financial abundance. You've got this, friend!

Very Next Action Steps

1. **Identify and confront your limiting beliefs:** Spend some time reflecting on your current beliefs about money and success. Write down any limiting beliefs you identify and confront them by examining where they came from and whether they truly serve you.

Be honest with yourself about how these beliefs may have held you back in the past, and commit to changing them.

2. **Replace limiting beliefs with empowering beliefs:** For each limiting belief you've identified, come up with an empowering belief that directly opposes it. Write these empowering beliefs down and commit to repeating them as daily affirmations. Over time, these positive statements will help to rewire your subconscious mind and replace your old limiting beliefs with new, empowering ones.

Resources: Go to ***unshakablewealth.com/affirm*** and download the *3D Affirmations To Unlock Your Full Potential Of Financial Success* guide to gain instant access to a powerful, proven affirmations framework specifically designed to rewire your brain for wealth, eliminating self-limiting beliefs and transforming your financial future.

2.2 - Crafting Powerful SMART Goals for Wealth and Abundance

"A goal properly set is halfway reached." - Zig Ziglar

Let's say you decided to go on a road trip. Would you pack your clothes, get in the car, and start driving without having an idea of where you are going? How would you know what to pack? What to take with you? Would you do that? No! You have a destination or at least an idea of where you are going. The goals are your destination and what you want to be and have.

It's crucial to set goals so you can live a life with direction. But goals only work if you are intentional and set them up correctly. Zig Ziglar nailed it when he said, "A goal properly set is halfway reached."

When pursuing your dreams, you're embarking on the adventure of a lifetime - a road trip with no limits, bound only by your wildest aspirations. Your journey to create a life of wealth and abundance begins here, in the driver's seat of your own destiny. But as with any great adventure, you need a destination, a roadmap, and the right tools to guide you along the way.

Goals are the key to unlocking your potential and creating a life that is truly aligned with your desires. They provide a sense of purpose, motivation, and direction, empowering you to make intentional decisions that shape your future. Without goals, it's all too easy to drift aimlessly through life, never quite reaching your full potential or manifesting the abundance you so deeply desire. Or worse, which happens to most people, you end up in a life you don't like, so far from your dreams that you are dreading it and want to escape. A life where you wake up in the morning and ask yourself, *Is this it? Being a grown-up isn't all that was hyped up to be.*

People drift in the whirlpool of routines, changed by responsibilities, and cruise through life in survival mode rather than thriving because of no direction and no clear vision of what they truly want.

We are all too familiar with the New Year resolutions and goals; many buy gym memberships, sign up for meal plans, and walk into the new year with "this is the year that I am going to rock." Yet, sadly, things fade away within a month and a half, about mid-February. Why?

In this fast-paced, ever-changing world, it's easy to lose sight of what truly matters and become mired in the daily grind. As we face mounting pressures, responsibilities, and expectations, our dreams and aspirations can become hazy, distant, and seemingly out of reach. But what if I told you that you have the power to transform your life, reclaim your dreams, and create a reality that is deeply fulfilling, meaningful, and abundant?

The key to unlocking this transformation lies in setting powerful SMART goals and cultivating winning habits that align with your values, purpose, and deepest desires. By doing so, you can reawaken the passion and drive that fuels your journey toward success, abundance, and true happiness.

When we set SMART goals deeply rooted in our core beliefs and values, we create a strong foundation for lasting change and transformation. These goals become a guiding light, a beacon that illuminates the path toward our ideal life, enabling us to navigate even the darkest, most challenging moments with grace, determination, and unwavering resolve.

By aligning our daily habits and actions with these goals, we make consistent progress toward our dreams and cultivate a deep sense of fulfillment, knowing that each step we take truly reflects our authentic selves. This sense of alignment, purpose, and congruence can be incredibly powerful, igniting a spark within us that fuels our transformation and propels us forward on our journey.

And that's why having goals is so important. But not all goals are created equal. Some are vague and nebulous, lacking the clarity and specificity to make them actionable. Others are unrealistic or unattainable, setting you up for disappointment and disillusionment. To create a life of true wealth and abundance, you need goals that are both inspiring and achievable — goals that are SMART.

I'm not talking about the kind of "smart" that requires a fancy degree or an Ivy League education. I'm talking about SMART goals — Specific, Measurable, Achievable, Relevant, and Time-bound. This simple yet powerful framework can transform how you approach goal setting, providing you with a crystal-clear roadmap to success.

Let's look at what it means to set SMART goals and how this approach can help you create a life of wealth and abundance.

Specific: A SMART goal is one that is clear and specific, not vague or confusing. It's not enough to say, "I want to be wealthy." Instead, you need to paint a vivid picture of what wealth looks like for you. How much money do you want to have in the bank? What kind of lifestyle do you want to lead? When your goals are specific, it's easier to create a plan of action and measure your progress along the way.

Measurable: A SMART goal is one that can be measured and tracked, allowing you to see your progress and make any necessary changes. This means breaking your goal down into smaller, quantifiable steps that can be easily monitored and assessed. For example, if your goal is to save $10,000 in one year, then you might break it down into monthly savings targets or weekly benchmarks. By making your goal measurable, you create a sense of accountability and momentum that propels you forward.

Achievable: A SMART goal is one that is realistic and attainable yet still challenging enough to inspire growth and transformation. It's important to achieve a balance between setting the bar too low and setting it so high that you become overwhelmed and discouraged. When setting your goals, consider your current resources, skills, and circumstances, as well as any potential obstacles or challenges that may arise. By setting achievable goals, you empower yourself to take consistent, focused action toward your desired outcome.

Relevant: A SMART goal is one that is relevant and aligned with your core values, passions, and aspirations. It's essential to ensure that your goals are meaningful and connected to your larger vision for your life. This fuels your motivation and helps you stay focused and committed, even when things get hard. When setting your goals, take the time to reflect on your deepest desires and ask yourself, *Is this goal truly aligned with the life I want to create?*

Time-bound: A SMART goal is one that has a clear deadline or timeframe, creating a sense of urgency and commitment. By giving yourself a specific timeline to work within, you establish a sense of structure and focus that can help you stay on track and prioritize your efforts.

Having a deadline also helps you maintain momentum and motivation, forcing you to take consistent action and make steady progress toward your goal. When setting your goals, be realistic about the timeframe, considering any potential obstacles or challenges that may arise. Remember, it's better to set a slightly flexible and achievable deadline rather than one that is too aggressive and unrealistic, leading to stress and disappointment.

Now that we've explored the elements of SMART goals, let's dive into some practical examples of how you can apply this framework to your own prosperity, wealth, and abundance journey.

Imagine your goal is to become financially independent within the next ten years. Using the SMART framework, you might define your goal as follows:

Specific: "I will build a passive income of $100,000 per year within ten years, allowing me to cover my living expenses and enjoy financial freedom."

Measurable: "I will track my progress by monitoring my monthly passive income, aiming to increase it by at least $833 per month ($10,000 per year)."

Achievable: "I will invest in income-producing assets, such as stocks, real estate, and small businesses, to generate the passive income needed to reach my goal."

Relevant: "Achieving financial independence aligns with my core values of freedom, security, and personal growth, enabling me to create a life of abundance and fulfillment on my own terms."

Time-bound: "I will reach my goal of $100,000 in annual passive income within ten years or by [specific date]."

By setting SMART goals like this, you can create a clear roadmap to wealth and abundance that is both inspiring and achievable. This fuels your motivation and helps you stay focused and committed when obstacles come your way.

In addition to setting SMART goals, developing and maintaining winning habits that support your journey to wealth and abundance is essential. Based on previous chapters, you already know that habits are a must in achieving success and play a crucial role in shaping your mindset, behavior, and, ultimately, your results.

As you continue pursuing your financial goals, consider the habits you can cultivate to support your journey. These might include:

1. Regularly reviewing and updating your goals to ensure they remain aligned with your evolving desires and circumstances.

2. Developing a consistent savings and investment plan that supports your wealth-building efforts.

3. Seeking out opportunities for personal and professional growth to enhance your skills and expand your network.

4. Surrounding yourself with like-minded individuals who inspire and challenge you to continue to grow and become the best version of yourself.

5. Practicing gratitude and mindfulness to cultivate a positive and abundant mindset.

By working towards your SMART goals and developing winning habits, you will start noticing profound changes in various aspects of your life. You may find that you are better equipped to handle stress, manage your time more effectively, and make decisions that align with your true values and aspirations. Your relationships may improve, your career may flourish, and your overall sense of well-being may soar to new heights.

The transformation that unfolds may surprise you and inspire those around you to embark on their own journeys of growth and self-discovery. This ripple effect can create a powerful, positive impact on your community, your loved ones, and the world at large.

As you embrace this transformational journey, patience and persistence are key. Building wealth, success, and abundance is a process that takes time, dedication, and unwavering commitment. There may be moments of doubt, fear, and uncertainty, but by staying true to your SMART goals and maintaining a steadfast focus on your vision, you can navigate these challenges and emerge stronger, more resilient, and more deeply connected to your purpose.

On this path of self-discovery and transformation, you may find that your journey takes unexpected twists and turns. Embrace these moments of uncertainty and change, for they are opportunities for growth, learning, and the chance to redefine what it means to live a truly prosperous life.

In these moments, when doubt and fear threaten to derail your progress, remind yourself of the incredible potential that lies within you. Remember the power of your "why," the driving force that fuels your passion and determination to create a life of wealth, abundance, and true success. Your "why" is your guiding star, your beacon in the storm, and the key to unlocking your full potential.

In your pursuit of a prosperous life, always remember the importance of balance and self-care. While staying focused and committed to your goals is essential, it's equally important to honor your physical, mental, and emotional needs. By nurturing all aspects of your well-being, you can ensure you have the energy, resilience, and inner strength to face whatever challenges life throws your way.

Celebrate your wins, both big and small, and take the time to appreciate the progress you've made along the way. Each step forward, no matter how seemingly insignificant, is a testament to your courage, determination, and commitment to creating a life of true wealth and abundance.

As you continue to build your unshakable wealth identity, you may find that your goals and aspirations evolve and change. This is a natural part of the journey and a sign that you are growing, learning, and expanding your horizons. Embrace these shifts and allow yourself the freedom and flexibility to adapt and redefine your vision of success and prosperity.

Ultimately, the path to a prosperous life is a deeply personal and individual journey. It's a voyage of self-discovery, growth, and transformation that will shape you into the person you are meant to become. Along the way, you will encounter challenges, setbacks, and moments of doubt, but you will also experience incredible triumphs, profound insights, and the joy of witnessing your dreams come to life.

So, take a deep breath, embrace your power of choice, and embark on this incredible journey with courage, conviction, and an unwavering belief in your own limitless potential. The life you've always dreamed of is waiting for you, and with each step you take, you move closer to making it a reality.

And as you continue to walk this path, remember that your prosperous life is not just about financial wealth and material abundance. It's about finding true fulfillment, happiness, and meaning in all aspects of your existence. It's about creating a life that aligns with your deepest values, passions, and dreams and discovering who you truly are and what you were meant to achieve in this world.

Don't take my word for it...

"With Lari's help, we became very clear about what we wanted out of life. Lari provided us with tools to monitor our progress and help keep us on track. We developed a specific, actionable plan to achieve our goals. We have a long-term wealth building and retirement plan that will benefit ourselves and our family for multiple generations to come, and we started looking for the home of our dreams. We were able to ramp up a stagnant real estate business that we operate on the side. The family now meets weekly to talk about life and business."

- Jimmy & Vanessa H.

Very Next Action Steps

1. **Define your goals:** Spend some time reflecting on your aspirations and what you want to achieve in life. Make a list of both short-term and long-term goals that follow your values and passions. Be as specific as possible in defining these goals to provide a clear direction for your journey.

2. **Make your goals SMART:** Transform your goals into SMART goals — Specific, Measurable, Achievable, Relevant, and Time-bound. This will ensure that your goals are clear, actionable, and realistic. Revisit and refine your goals to maintain relevance to your evolving life circumstances.

3. **Create an action plan:** Break down your SMART goals into smaller, manageable steps or milestones. Develop a detailed action plan outlining the tasks and timelines required to achieve each goal. Regularly review and make necessary changes to your action plan to keep yourself on track and accountable for your progress.

2.3 - Design a Progress-Tracking System

"What gets measured gets managed, what gets managed gets results." - Larisa Olteanu

Imagine it's a typical Monday morning, and you're already feeling overwhelmed by the long list of tasks you need to accomplish this week. You know you want to make progress on your goals and establish new habits, but with so many competing priorities, it's hard to know where to start or how to measure your progress. Suddenly, it feels like your dreams are slipping through your fingers, and your goals and habits become an afterthought. Can you relate? I bet you can. I've been there, and I'm sure you've been there, too. It's easy to lose yourself in the day-to-day grind and lose sight of our long-term dreams and aspirations.

That's where a progress-tracking system comes into play. It's a tool that will help you stay focused on your goals, monitor your habits, and celebrate your achievements along the way. Remember, life is about choices, and the progress-tracking system will help you make more informed and empowered choices as you journey toward a prosperous life.

When I first moved to the United States, I dreamed of building a successful career and creating a better life for my family. However, with so many responsibilities and distractions, it was easy to lose sight of my goals. I chose to be proactive and take control of my life by designing a progress-tracking system that allowed me to stay focused on my goals and habits. And by doing that, I could visualize my achievements, identify areas for improvement, and stay motivated even when life got tough. And it worked! I went from being a server with limited English skills to a finance professional at a Fortune 500 and the top publicly traded energy company, and a proud mom pursuing an MBA at the University of Texas, McCombs School of Business while building my wealth portfolio.

So, let's dive in and cover how you can design a progress-tracking system that works for you. But first, let's tackle the big elephant in the room: why do we need a progress-tracking system in the first place? The answer is simple — what gets measured gets managed. If you don't track your progress, staying motivated, maintaining momentum, and understanding what's working and what's not is difficult. It's crucial to stay focused and adapt our strategies when necessary. Tracking our progress allows us to do just that.

Here is how to design a progress-tracking system that fits your unique needs and preferences:

1. **Take your goals and habits:** The first step in designing a progress-tracking system is to take the identified SMART goals and the habits you want to develop and think about the big picture and the smaller steps that will help you get there. For example, if your SMART goal is to achieve financial freedom, you might focus on habits like saving a portion of your income, investing regularly, and cutting unnecessary expenses.

2. **Break your goals into smaller milestones:** Big goals can be intimidating, so breaking them down into smaller, manageable milestones is essential. This will make tracking your progress more straightforward and help you stay motivated as you celebrate each achievement along the way. Remember when I stayed in the United States with only $20 in my pocket and a dream to build a better life?

By breaking down my goals into smaller steps and aligning them with daily habits, I navigated the challenges and made significant progress toward success.

3. **Choose a tracking method that works for you:** There are countless ways to track your progress, so choose a method that resonates with you and your lifestyle. Some prefer digital tools like spreadsheets or mobile apps, while others opt for a good old-fashioned pen and paper. Experiment with different tracking methods and find one you enjoy using and can commit to regularly.

4. **Make tracking a daily habit:** Consistency is key to making progress toward your goals and establishing new habits. Set aside a few minutes daily to update your progress-tracking system, reflecting on what went well and where you can improve. This daily practice will help you stay motivated and focused even when things get hard.

5. **Monitor your progress and adjust your strategy:** Your progress-tracking system isn't just a way to record your achievements; it's also a tool to help you learn and grow. Regularly review your progress and look for patterns and trends to help you adjust your strategy. Are you constantly struggling with a particular habit? Maybe it's time to try a different approach or seek support from a mentor or accountability partner.

6. **Celebrate your wins and learn from setbacks:** It's essential to acknowledge and celebrate your progress, no matter how small. Each milestone reached brings you closer to your ultimate goal. When you achieve a milestone or develop a new habit, take a moment to appreciate your hard work and dedication. Celebrating your achievements will boost your motivation and reinforce your commitment to your goals.

Remember, setbacks are inevitable, but they're also valuable learning opportunities. Don't be too hard on yourself when you face challenges or slip-ups. Instead, use these experiences to gain insights and refine your approach. Remember that progress isn't always linear, and it's okay to stumble as long as you pick yourself up and keep moving forward.

7. **Share your progress with others:** Sharing your goals and progress with others can be a powerful motivator and provide you with a valuable support system. This can be done by discussing your goals with friends or family members, joining a group of like-minded individuals, or connecting with an accountability partner. By sharing your journey, you'll benefit from encouragement, advice, and a sense of camaraderie that can help you stay focused and committed.

8. **Regularly review and update your goals:** As you make progress toward your goals, it's crucial to review and reassess them periodically. This will help you ensure your goals align with your values, priorities, and long-term vision. It's also an opportunity to set new goals, adjust your habits, and refine your strategies based on your experiences and insights.

In conclusion, designing a progress-tracking system is a powerful way to stay focused on your goals, develop healthy habits, and celebrate your achievements. By identifying your goals and habits, breaking them down into manageable milestones, and tracking your progress consistently, you'll be closer than most people to accomplishing your dream life.

Don't take my word for it...

"I come from a family of teachers and farmers in rural Kansas who've never had any wealth in their families. I resonated with how little (Lari) came from and how hard she worked to educate herself and build a life different from the one she was born into. I know what kind of internal work is required to achieve small milestones, and it's admirable to see people accomplish their lofty goals. I was excited to learn from someone who'd already done the work to develop a healthy mindset around building wealth. I have negotiated pay for the first time, learned exactly how my work has contributed value – building a resilient confidence in me. Lari sped up my timeline, and now my confidence in myself has grown 10x. It took me adapting my mindset, consistently making small changes, and building healthy habits."

- Megan S.

Very Next Action Steps

1. **Set aside time to break each goal into smaller milestones:** This makes them less overwhelming and more manageable. Consider the habits you'll need to align or develop to support these goals.

2. **Choose your tracking method and create your system:** Based on your preferences and lifestyle, decide on a tracking method that resonates with you, whether it's a digital tool like a spreadsheet or mobile app, or pen and paper. Create a progress-tracking system that includes your goals, habits, and milestones, and make it visually appealing and easy to use.

3. **Commit to daily tracking and reflection:** Set a designated time every day to update your progress-tracking system, ideally at the end of the

day when you can reflect on what went well and where you can improve. This is a nonnegotiable part of your daily success routine. As you update your tracking system, celebrate your achievements, learn from setbacks, and adjust your strategies as needed to stay focused and motivated on your journey towards your goals.

Resources: Get the Goal progress-tracking Sheet here: ***unshakablewealth.com/bookgifts***

CHAPTER 3

Fostering a Prosperous Mindset

3.1 - Harness the Power of Vision Boards for a Rich Life

"The power of imagination makes us infinite." - John Muir

You know, I still remember the day when I was only 14 years old, sitting in our tiny bedroom with a pair of scissors, stacks of magazines, and a piece of white A4 paper. I was creating my very first vision board, and little did I know, it would be the beginning of a lifelong practice that has helped me manifest the most amazing experiences and accomplishments in my life.

Inspired by my love for American movies, I crafted my very own vision board, placing the iconic Hollywood sign in the center as a symbol of my dream to one day travel to Los Angeles, California.

I added pictures of the world's most beautiful beaches, as I wanted to experience luxurious vacations in exotic destinations like Bora Bora and the Maldives. I allowed my dreams to soar, free from the limitations that sometimes held me back in the poorest country in Europe.

Little did I know my vision board would come to life in ways I could never have imagined. Fast forward years later, and I'm living out many of the visions I placed on that board — from traveling to breathtaking destinations like Bora

Bora and the Maldives to marrying a talented chef who has brought so much joy and love into my life.

You may be wondering, *What's the big deal about vision boards? How can a bunch of images and words pasted onto a piece of cardboard really make a difference in your life?* The answer lies in the power of visualization.

One remarkable aspect of the human mind is its ability to visualize and imagine the future. When we create a vision board, we bring those dreams to life, creating a tangible representation of our desires and aspirations. This powerful tool allows us to focus our minds on the things that truly matter to us and motivates us to pursue our dreams relentlessly.

A vision board is created using images, words, and other elements arranged on a cork board, poster board, or a digital board created in a Word document. The purpose of a vision board is not merely to "manifest" your desires or rely on "the law of attraction." Instead, it serves as a daily reminder to help your brain focus on what truly matters to you.

Your brain houses this incredible feature called the reticular activating system (RAS), which is like the VIP bouncer of your thoughts. It filters out the distractions and lets only the important stuff through. Keeping your vision board front and center gives your RAS the heads up on what you really want to focus on. That constant visual reminder helps your subconscious stay locked on your goals, so you're doing mini visualization and goal-setting exercises throughout the day, often without even realizing it. How cool is that?

So even if you initially think, "I don't believe in visualization techniques," or "I don't see the value in creating a vision board," give it a chance, and you might be surprised at the powerful impact it can have on your life. Remember, what you focus on expands. A vision board offers a tangible way to visualize your goals and cultivate the mindset to achieve them daily.

When you create a vision board, you're tapping into your brain's incredible ability to create vivid mental pictures of the experiences, possessions, and achievements you desire. By visualizing your goals this way, you're training your brain to recognize and seize opportunities that will bring you closer to making those dreams a reality.

When you see an image of that dream house, beach vacation, or successful business on your vision board daily, you're planting a seed in your subconscious mind. Over time, that seed starts to grow and flourish, influencing your thoughts, beliefs, and actions in ways that align with your goals.

Think about it. Before airplanes took flight, cities rose, houses were built, or rockets launched, each of these incredible achievements started as an idea in someone's mind. They began as a visualized drawing on paper, just like the ones you'll create on your vision board. After all, you wouldn't hire a construction crew without having a solid idea of what you're building, right?

So, how does one go about creating a vision board? The process is simple but requires intention and focus. Start with your written goals and dreams and the questions we explored in the previous chapters. What do you want to achieve in life? What kind of experiences do you want to have? What kind of person do you want to be? These questions will help guide you as you create your vision board.

Next, gather materials that represent your goals and dreams. This can include photographs, magazine clippings, inspirational quotes, and anything else that resonates with you. Be creative and have fun with this process — the more personal your vision board, the more powerful it will be.

Arrange the materials on a poster board or corkboard in a way that feels right to you. There are no rules when creating a vision board — the most important thing is that it resonates with you and motivates you to pursue your dreams.

Once your vision board is done, hang it in a place where you'll see it every day. This constant reminder of your goals and dreams will help keep you focused and motivated as you work towards a richer, more prosperous life.

Creating a vision board is not just about assembling images and materials representing your desires. It's about taking the time to reflect on what you truly want in life and committing to making those dreams a reality. This introspective process can be incredibly transformative and empowering.

As you look at your vision board each day, you'll begin to internalize your dreams and develop an unshakeable belief in your ability to achieve them. You'll also start to notice opportunities and resources that can help you reach your goals — things you may not have noticed before.

The power of visualization is not to be underestimated. Studies have shown that the act of visualizing a desired outcome can improve performance and increase the likelihood of achieving a goal. Our minds are incredibly powerful, and when we focus on our dreams, we unlock the potential to create the life we've always wanted.

Incorporating a vision board into your daily routine is an excellent way to foster a prosperous mindset. It's a constant reminder of your goals and dreams, helping you stay focused and motivated on your journey to wealth and abundance.

Very Next Action Steps

1. **Have your written goals:** Have your written goals in front of you, as they will serve as the foundation for your vision board.

2. **Gather materials and create your vision board:** Find images, quotes, and other elements representing your goals and dreams. Use photographs, magazine clippings, or even create digital images. Be

creative and have fun with this process, ensuring your vision board is personal and powerful. Arrange the materials on a poster board, corkboard, or digital board in a way that resonates with you and motivates you to pursue your dreams.

3. **Display your vision board and engage with it daily:** Hang your vision board in an obvious place where you'll see it every day. Spend a few minutes each day looking at your vision board and visualizing yourself achieving your goals.

3.2 - Embrace a Gratitude System for Lasting Fulfillment

"Gratitude is not only the greatest of virtues but the parent of all others."
- Marcus Tullius

Let me tell you about a life-transforming realization I made that forever changed how I approach my journey toward a prosperous life. It's a secret ingredient we all know about, but don't practice enough, and adds flavor, richness, and meaning to every aspect of our lives.

It's gratitude.

Yes, you read that right. Gratitude can create a lasting impact on your fulfillment, happiness, and overall well-being. It's one of the most significant building blocks of a prosperous mindset. And, before your mind says, "Duh, I know this, not a groundbreaking discovery." I want to challenge you with the following question: When was the last time you took the time out of your day to be thankful for the things in life that are taken for granted (i.e., the gift of life, your ability to see, hear, smell, taste, your family, your clean sheets, clean water to drink, a hot shower)? When was the last time you sat down with someone or wrote someone a note to tell them how much they impacted your life?

It's easy at the surface to say, "Yeah, I know, I am grateful," but it's much harder to be honest with yourself, embody, model, live and breathe gratitude every day of your life.

It's also natural to face challenges like difficulty shifting focus to a prosperous mindset, lack of consistency in practicing gratitude, or an inability to recognize the good in every situation. You might also feel overwhelmed and stressed by life, lack fulfillment and joy, or struggle to maintain a positive outlook.

Gratitude is a powerful force for change. Take a diamond, which is a dirty rock in some cave. As that rock is picked up and run through a machine to apply pressure and polish it, it turns into a clear object radiating brilliance. Those who practice gratitude for every situation and learning in life turn into brilliance.

Before diving into the beauty and magic of gratitude, let me share a story with you. When I lived in the U.S., I struggled to adapt to the culture and the new environment. I met this wonderful couple, Danny and Teresa, their interview is included at the end of the book. Danny, a very successful real estate investor, inspired me to what one can achieve in the U.S. Danny & Teresa motivated me to want more, do more and be more. As my life unfolded, they were there for me in many moments of need. They were the only ones who came to my bachelor's degree graduation ceremony besides my husband and stepson. This was a very touching moment as I watched the rest of my classmates being celebrated by fathers, mothers, brothers, cousins, and many other friends and family.

Their presence in my life continued with Danny mentoring me through my real estate investment journey, sharing his contacts, and sometimes stopping by remodeling sights to see how things were going. Our paths split, and for years, we didn't see each other as often. Even though I said many times,

"Thank you" in those moments, I knew that I needed to sit down, look them both in the eyes and thank them for all they had done for me, show them my deep, heartfelt gratitude for who they are and how much they meant to me. So, I made an intentional choice and did exactly that. And it was then that I realized how grateful I was for them and the person I was becoming. My life has never been the same since I started to embrace gratitude.

You might wonder why gratitude plays a significant role in building a prosperous mindset. Well, it's simple: when you're grateful for what you have, you're more likely to appreciate the journey and focus on the positives rather than the negatives. This attitude shift can make all the difference in your ability to overcome challenges, stay motivated, and ultimately achieve your goals.

Think about it. When you're grateful, you're more likely to see the opportunities in every situation. You become a magnet for abundance because your positive mindset attracts more of what you want in life. And the best part? Regardless of where you are on your wealth and prosperity journey, this practice doesn't cost a thing, and it's available to everyone.

Gratitude is the key that unlocks lasting fulfillment. It's not just about being thankful for the big moments but also for the little things in life that make it beautiful, memorable, and worth living. It's about recognizing the good that exists in every situation and acknowledging the people who support us in our journey.

So, how do we embrace a gratitude system for lasting fulfillment? Let's explore this idea together.

First and foremost, understand that gratitude is a choice. It's a conscious decision we make to focus on the positive things in our lives, even when things seem to be falling apart. Remember my story about standing up to my abusive stepfather? That was a choice I made that ultimately saved my mom's life and set me on the path to a better future. Choosing to be grateful in every situation can be a powerful catalyst for transformation, development, and abundance.

One way to make gratitude a habit is to practice it daily. You can start each day by taking a moment to think about what you're grateful for. It can be as simple as being thankful for a warm bed to sleep in, a loving family, or a job that allows you to pursue your dreams. You can even keep a gratitude journal, where you jot down three things you're grateful for daily. This practice will help you focus on the positive and attract more abundance and prosperity into your life.

Another way to embrace gratitude is to express it to others. We often take the people in our lives for granted, assuming they know how much we appreciate them. But, by genuinely expressing our gratitude to them, we make them feel valued, strengthen our relationships, and build a solid support system. Make it a point to thank people who have helped you, inspired you, or made your day better.

Furthermore, we can cultivate gratitude by giving back to our community. We gain a deep sense of fulfillment and purpose when we help others and make a difference in their lives. Volunteering, mentoring, or even just lending a listening ear to someone in need can create a ripple effect of gratitude and positivity in the world around us.

It's also essential to practice self-gratitude. Often, we are our own harshest critics, focusing on our flaws and failures instead of celebrating our achievements and strengths. Take time to acknowledge your wins and accomplishments, even if they seem small, and be kind to yourself.

Creating Your Gratitude System

Now that we've established the importance of gratitude in fostering a prosperous mindset, let's talk about how you can create your own Gratitude

System. This system is not a one-size-fits-all approach but rather a framework that can be tailored to fit your unique needs, preferences, and lifestyle. Here's a simple step-by-step guide to help you create a Gratitude System that works for you:

1. **List 3-5 things daily:** Write down 3-5 things you're grateful for each day. These can be big or small, such as a delicious cup of coffee, a beautiful sunset, and a supportive friend.

2. **Go beyond the surface:** As you list your gratitude, try to dig deeper and identify why you're grateful for each item. For example, if you're grateful for a friend, think about the specific qualities they possess that make you appreciate them.

3. **Reflect on challenges:** Recognize that even difficult situations can provide opportunities for growth and gratitude. Consider the lessons you've learned from challenges and how they've shaped you into a stronger person.

4. **Share your gratitude:** Express your appreciation to others, whether it's through a heartfelt thank you, a thoughtful note, or a simple gesture. This strengthens your relationships and reinforces your gratitude practice.

5. **Be present:** Practice mindfulness by focusing on the present moment and savoring the positive experiences in your life. This can help you be more conscious of the things you're grateful for.

6. **Cultivate a gratitude mindset:** As you continue your gratitude practice, try incorporating this mindset into other aspects of your life. In every situation, look for the good and appreciate the beautiful world around you.

7. **Revisit your gratitude journal:** Periodically review your past entries to remind yourself of the many things you are grateful for. This can be especially helpful during difficult times, providing a sense of perspective and resilience.

Embracing a gratitude system is a powerful and transformative approach to cultivating a prosperous mindset. When we consciously choose to focus on the positives in our lives and express our appreciation for the people and experiences that shape us, we invite lasting fulfillment, happiness, and well-being. By making gratitude a daily practice, not only do we enrich our own lives, but we also create a ripple effect of positivity and abundance in the world around us. As we navigate the path toward prosperity, let us remember to cherish the journey, acknowledge our accomplishments, and be grateful for the support and love of those around us. Ultimately, a heart filled with gratitude is the foundation for a truly prosperous life.

Very Next Action Steps

1. **Start a Gratitude Journal:** Begin your day by writing down three to five things you're grateful for. This simple act helps you focus on the positive aspects of your life and shifts your mindset towards abundance and prosperity. As you continue this practice, you will notice a greater sense of fulfillment and happiness.

2. **Express Gratitude to Others:** Make a conscious effort to genuinely thank the people who have made a difference in your life, whether they are friends, family, or mentors. Sharing your appreciation strengthens your relationships and reinforces your gratitude practice, creating a cycle of positivity and abundance.

3. **Give Back to Your Community:** Find opportunities to impact other people's lives by helping them. This could be through volunteering,

mentoring, or simply offering a listening ear to someone in need. By giving back, you cultivate a deeper sense of gratitude and create a positive ripple effect in the world around you.

3.3 - Cultivate an Effective Daily Success Routine

"The greatest glory in living lies not in never falling, but in rising every time we fall." - Nelson Mandela

Imagine you're standing at the base of a magnificent mountain, looking up at the peak that seems to touch the sky. You've spent weeks studying climbing techniques, learning about the terrain, and listening to the advice of experienced mountaineers. As you take your first step on the trail, you realize that you have the power within you to overcome any obstacle and reach the summit. And so, you begin your climb.

Life is a lot like that mountain. We all have unique skills, experiences, and knowledge acquired from various sources, but it's up to us to face the challenges and harness these qualities in our daily lives.

Now, close your eyes and envision your perfect day. What does it look like? From the moment you open your eyes to when you tuck yourself in at night, how are you spending your time? Are you focused on the right things, developing the right habits, and nurturing the right mindset to achieve your wealth goals?

In this section, we'll explore practical ways to create a daily success routine that combines your new wealth identity, SMART goals, vision board, and gratitude system, as well as your habits and limiting beliefs. The goal is to design a routine that empowers you to make the most of every day, propelling you forward on your journey to unshakable wealth.

Remember, life is about choices. The choice to step forward to climb the mountain and create the life you've always imagined is yours to make. So, let's dive into crafting your effective daily success routine.

First things first, let's talk about the importance of intentionality. To create a daily routine that aligns with your wealth goals, you must be intentional about the choices you make and the activities you engage in. Begin each day by setting your intention, focusing on what matters most to you, and then aligning your actions with your purpose.

One of the key aspects of cultivating an effective daily success routine is understanding that no two routines will look the same. You're a unique individual with your own goals, dreams, and priorities. Your routine should reflect that. So, let's dive in and create a tailor-made daily success routine that combines everything you've learned so far.

First and foremost, start your day with intention. Make a conscious decision to focus on your new wealth identity and your unstoppable "why." Each morning be intentional and take a moment to remind yourself of the powerful habits you're building and the goals you're working towards. This mental preparation will set the stage for a successful day.

Next, review your vision board. Take a few minutes each morning to visualize the life you would love waking up to and want to create for yourself. This daily practice will help you stay connected to your dreams and keep you motivated as you work toward them. Don't let fear limit your imagination — let it run wild! The more vivid and exciting the vision, the more energized and committed you'll be to achieving it.

Now, it's time to express gratitude. Every day take some time to reflect on the things you're grateful for. Nothing complicated; simply jot down three things you're thankful for in a journal or a more elaborate ritual involving meditation or prayer. The important thing is to make gratitude a regular part of your daily routine. When you do, you'll find that your mindset shifts from scarcity to abundance.

With your mind focused on your goals and your heart filled with gratitude, it's time to get to work. Break down your long-term SMART goals into smaller, actionable steps. Each day, identify the specific tasks you need to complete to make progress toward your goals. It's important to be realistic and not overload yourself — remember that this is a marathon, not a sprint. Stay committed to your tasks, but also be flexible and open to alter your plans as needed.

As you conquer those daily tasks, be mindful of the habits you're cultivating. Are they serving your new wealth identity? Are they helping you move closer to your goals? If not, it's time to reassess and make changes. Remember, your habits are the building blocks of your success. Be intentional about fostering habits that align with your goals and dreams.

Throughout the day, take breaks to recharge and reflect. This might mean stepping away from your desk for a quick walk or spending a few minutes in quiet meditation. The key is to give yourself permission to pause and re-center. By doing so, you'll maintain your focus and energy, making it easier to stay on track with your daily success routine.

Set aside time for reflection and relaxation as you wrap up your day. Review your accomplishments and celebrate your wins, no matter how small they may seem. Acknowledging your progress boosts your self-esteem and motivation, helping you pinpoint areas where you can improve or adjust your approach.

Before you go to bed, take a few minutes to plan for the next day. Write down your priorities, tasks, and any appointments or commitments. Doing this will prepare you to hit the ground running when you wake up, ensuring you stay focused and productive.

Finally, practice self-care to maintain your mental and physical well-being. Eat a balanced diet, get a good night's sleep, and participate in things that fill you up with joy and relax you. A healthy mind and body are imperative for sustaining the energy and resilience needed to achieve wealth-building goals.

Incorporating these elements into your daily success routine will create a powerful foundation for success. Remember, the key to lasting change is consistency. Stick to your routine, stay focused on your goals, and remain open to growth and learning.

As you refine and improve your daily success routine, remember that you are destined for wealth, and the power to create unshakable wealth lies within you. Like a mountain climb, it's up to you to harness your skills, knowledge, and experiences to make the most of every day and achieve the life of your dreams. So, take a deep breath and step into the limitless possibilities that await you.

PHASE 2

Money Management System

"Control your money, or it will control you; effective money management is the foundation upon which lasting wealth and financial freedom are built." - Larisa Olteanu

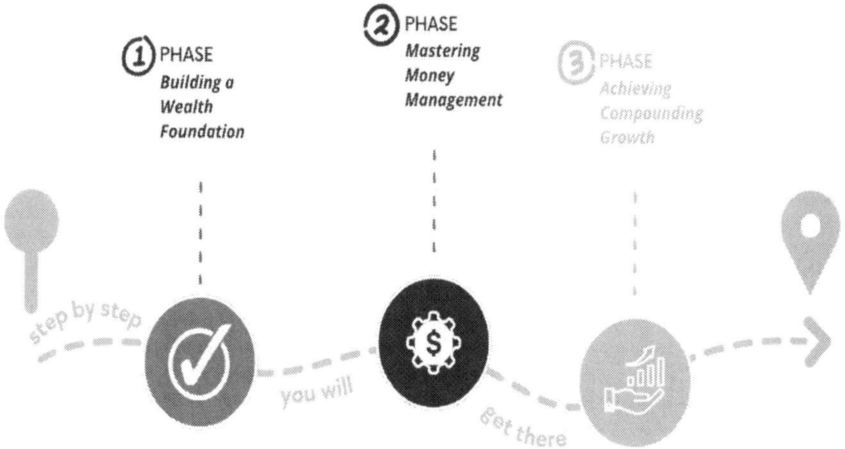

CHAPTER 4

Optimized Value-Based Spending

4.1 - Establish a money tracking system

"By harnessing the power of money tracking, you transform your finances into a well-tuned machine, driving with precision and purpose towards the ultimate destination of financial success, where dreams become reality and possibilities become limitless." - Larisa Olteanu

Think about the last time you felt sick and didn't know what was wrong. You probably tried to fix it yourself with over-the-counter meds, but in the end, you got the advice of a medical professional who could diagnose your condition and prescribe the appropriate treatment. Similar to determining the correct remedy for your sickness, you need to understand where you stand before you can come up with a plan to build wealth.

The purpose of a money tracking system is twofold: first, to find out where your money is slipping away, and second, to understand and monitor your net worth. By implementing a money-tracking system and getting a handle on both things, you can begin your wealth-building journey with a clear understanding of your current financial standing, putting you way closer to achieving financial success.

Let's explore the first objective of a money tracking system: identifying money flow drainages. Everyone has areas in their financial lives where money seems to disappear, and these drainages must be addressed. Knowing where your money is going and actively tracking its flow is crucial. For example, one of my clients, Bogdan, was spending $1,000 per month eating out without even realizing it. After implementing a money tracking system, he reduced this spending by $600 per month, saving him $7,200 per year while still enjoying the things he loves.

There are two primary methods for setting up a money tracking system: using an online platform, I prefer Empower.com, or manually tracking your finances using a spreadsheet. Regardless of the method you choose, both approaches will help you understand your income, expenses, investments, net worth, and debt, putting you on the path toward financial success.

To begin using a money tracking system, start by reviewing your income and expenses for the past three months. Examine your bank and credit card statements and any cash transactions so you can clearly understand your financial activity during this period. This initial analysis will help you identify areas of financial leakage and provide a clear focus for improvement.

The second objective of a money-tracking system is understanding and tracking your net worth. The term "net worth" may sound complicated, but it is straightforward. To calculate your net worth, take the value of everything you own and subtract your outstanding debts. For example, if you own a car worth $15,000 and have $2,000 in your bank account but owe $10,000 on a car loan, your net worth would be $7,000 ($15,000 + $2,000 - $10,000).

If you use an online platform with a feature to track your net worth, these calculations will be done automatically. Some of my students prefer using The Ultimate Annual Spending Plan spreadsheet, which tracks the net worth and helps build a comprehensive annual wealth plan. An online platform or a spreadsheet will allow you to track your financial progress and ensure you're heading in the right direction in your wealth-building journey.

By implementing a money-tracking system and consistently having a pulse on your financial health, you can make more educated decisions about your spending, saving, and investing habits. This level of financial awareness will empower you to take control of your money and make strategic choices that support your long-term financial goals. Additionally, understanding your net worth provides a clear benchmark for measuring your progress, giving you the motivation and confidence to stay committed to your wealth-building journey.

As you progress in your financial journey, regularly reviewing and updating your money-tracking system is crucial. By staying engaged with your finances and adapting your approach, you can ensure your wealth-building plan remains relevant and effective. This ongoing engagement with your finances will help you cultivate healthy money habits that support long-term financial success.

Remember that the path to financial freedom is not a one-time effort; it requires consistent attention, dedication, and patience. You will witness the results of your hard work as you refine your money-tracking system and optimize your spending, saving, and investing decisions. Your net worth will grow, your financial confidence will improve, and you will be well on your way to achieving financial success to get you closer to your dreams.

It's also important to recognize that financial setbacks are a natural part of the wealth-building process. Unexpected expenses, market fluctuations, and changes in circumstances may temporarily derail your progress, but don't let these challenges discourage you. By maintaining a robust money-tracking system and staying committed to your financial goals, you can weather these storms and emerge even stronger.

As the ancient Chinese philosopher Lao Tzu said, "A journey of a thousand miles begins with a single step." By implementing a money tracking system and taking control of your financial health, you are taking that first crucial step towards a future of financial freedom. With perseverance, determination, and the right tools, you can overcome obstacles, build lasting wealth, and secure a more abundant future for yourself and your loved ones.

Remember that knowledge is not power — ACTION is power!

Very Next Action Steps

1. **Choose a money-tracking method:** Decide whether you want to use a spreadsheet or use an online platform like Empower.com or manually track your finances. Whichever you pick, make sure it works for you, and you can consistently update.

2. **Analyze your past three months of income and expenses:** Go through your bank and credit card statements and any cash transactions from the past three months. This will help you identify areas where money is slipping away and give you a clearer focus on where you need to make improvements.

3. **Calculate and track your net worth.**

4.2 - Ditch Traditional Budgeting for Value-Based Spending

"Live well, spend wisely, and cherish the journey to financial freedom." - Larisa Olteanu

Ditch the boundaries of traditional budgeting; embrace an optimized spending plan that aligns with your core values, enriches your well-being, and paves the way to financial success without sacrificing the joys of today.

With all its benefits, the traditional budget often falls short of helping people achieve financial freedom. Budgets can be stifling, restrictive, and counterproductive to a fulfilling life. The reason? They may require you to sacrifice the things you enjoy, which can have a negative impact on your mind, spirit, and body. There is a better way: an optimized spending plan aligned with your personal values. This gives you the power and confidence to take control of your spending without compromising on the things you love and bring you joy.

An optimized spending plan is not a budget. While a budget focuses on cutting costs and penny-pinching, a spending plan prioritizes your spending to get the most out of your money. It acknowledges that not all spending is harmful and that sacrificing what you love can be detrimental to your well-being. The key is to align your spending with your core values, ensuring that your money is being used in ways that truly matter to you.

Creating a spending plan begins with an organized dashboard that offers a big-picture view of your finances, which we covered in detail in the previous section. Though it requires some initial time and effort to set up, the dashboard allows you to track your spending habits and monitor your net worth. This visibility into your financial life is critical to making more informed and intentional decisions about where your money goes.

The first step in building an optimized spending plan is to eliminate destructive expenses, such as bank fees, late fees, and other expenses that don't align with your five core values. Hang on tight because, in the next section of this chapter, we will cover in detail how to identify your core values. By cutting waste and focusing on what you value most, you can ensure your money is used wisely and purposefully.

Next, focus on consumption expenses, which can be divided into needs and wants. "Needs" expenses, like housing, bills, and insurance, are necessary for daily living and should account for approximately 50% of your take-home pay. While many "needs" expenses cannot be cut, they can often be lowered, which we will cover in the next chapter.

On the other hand, "wants" are expenses you can live without but choose to indulge in. Examples include the latest gadgets, streaming services, and designer clothes. Use your five core values as a guide to determine which ones to keep and which to eliminate. When considering large expenses, think long-term and weigh your options through the lens of your core values. If an item still serves its purpose two years from now, you can feel better about purchasing it. However, if you anticipate losing interest in the item within that time frame, it may be best to pass on it.

The final category of expenses to consider in your spending plan is "peace of mind" expenses. Often overlooked, these expenses are crucial to ensuring a more joyful life. Examples include health, home, and car insurance, life insurance, emergency preparedness, food storage, and long-term disability coverage. While many of these expenses cannot be cut, they can often be lowered.

The objective of an optimized spending plan is not to deprive yourself but to align your expenses with your core values. By focusing on what brings the most value to your life and being conscious of your money flow, you can enjoy life now and still build wealth for the future, ultimately achieving true financial freedom.

In a world where budgeting has long been touted as the answer to financial success, it's essential to recognize the limitations of this approach. Restrictive budgets can be unhealthy for the mind, spirit, and body, leading to dissatisfaction and unfulfilled desires. In contrast, an optimized spending plan aligned with personal values empowers you to take control of — your spending without sacrificing what you love. By prioritizing the things that are important to you, you can enjoy life today without sacrificing your financial future. Embrace this approach and discover a more fulfilling path to financial freedom that prioritizes your well-being and values above all else.

Very Next Action Steps

1. **Identify and eliminate destructive expenses:** Review your financial dashboard and identify any expenses that do not align with your core values and those that are unnecessary or wasteful. Make a plan to eliminate or reduce these expenses to optimize your spending.

2. **Evaluate your needs and wants:** Analyze your consumption expenses and categorize them into needs and wants. Assess your "needs" expenses to see if any can be lowered. This will help you determine which "wants" are meaningful and which can be eliminated or reduced, allowing you to prioritize spending aligning with your values.

4.3 - Align Spending with Core Values and Enjoy What Matters

"Align your spending with your values to enjoy life today while still building for tomorrow." - Larisa Olteanu

In a world of constant noise and a multitude of messages about what we should and shouldn't spend our money on, it's easy to get caught up in feeling guilty about our spending choices. Society has conditioned us to view spending as a negative, often leaving us with feelings of doubt, regret, and anxiety. However, not all spending is inherently bad. The key to making sound financial decisions is spending according to our values. This chapter will explore the concept of value spending and how it can transform your financial life.

Value spending is understanding the distinction between price, cost, and value. It's about making intentional spending decisions based on what matters most to you. When you engage in value spending, you track your expenses to ensure you're not living beyond your means and to create opportunities to allocate your resources toward the things you truly value.

We live in a world where financial gurus often shame us for our spending choices. Some people will tell you spending money on a daily cup of coffee, a luxurious vacation, or organic groceries is frivolous. However, what matters most is not what others think but what you believe is important based on your values. Your personal values should dictate where you choose to allocate your resources.

By tracking your expenses, you will gain insight into what you value. For example, if you value your health, you may find that a significant portion of your expenses are directed toward organic food, gym memberships, and other wellness-related activities. If you value experiences and personal growth, you might prioritize allocating funds toward travel or personal development courses. The key is to spend on what truly adds value to your life, whether it be that morning cup of coffee that brings you joy and increases your productivity or a memorable vacation with your family.

Wealthy individuals often prioritize value over cost or price when making spending decisions. By focusing on the value of a purchase, they can create a life that aligns with their priorities and goals. For instance, if you value your family's health and the creation of lasting memories, you may choose to forego eating out, luxury cars, or brand-name clothing to purchase organic food and travel. When your expenses reflect your values, you're more likely to experience greater fulfillment and satisfaction in your financial choices.

The concept of Value-Based Spending empowers you to enjoy life now while planning for the future. So, how can you begin to optimize your spending based on your values?

- *The first step* is tracking your expenses, as discussed in the previous section.

- *The second step* is to identify your core values, which should be limited to no more than five. Take your time in this process, and be intentional about what matters most to you. For example, your core values might include spirituality, family, health, service, and wealth.

- *The third step* in optimizing your value spending is to examine your expenses and determine which ones align with your values and which do not. For instance, if a Netflix subscription doesn't align with any of your core values, it might be time to cancel it. However, if self-development books align with your spirituality, family, and wealth values, investing in them makes sense.

As you progress toward financial success, remember that embracing value spending doesn't mean you must eliminate all indulgences or pleasures. It's about making intentional choices that align with your values and support your financial goals. Doing so will cultivate a deeper sense of fulfillment, satisfaction, and peace with your financial life.

By adopting the principles of value spending, you're no longer a passive recipient of society's expectations but an active participant in shaping your financial destiny. You hold the power to create a life that reflects your unique values and, in turn, build a foundation for lasting financial success and freedom. As you begin this journey, you will discover that your relationship with money evolves into a more positive and empowering one, where you consciously choose to spend on what truly enriches your life.

When we align our spending with our values, we are better equipped to make meaningful decisions that support our financial goals and overall well-being. This alignment can lead to a profound sense of satisfaction, as we are no longer chasing after the fleeting happiness that comes from short-term pleasures or following societal expectations. Instead, we invest in ourselves, our families, and our futures by making choices that honor what we hold dear.

As you refine and optimize your value spending, you may find that some of your values evolve over time. This is natural and reflects the dynamic nature of life. Stay attuned to these shifts and be willing to reassess your spending choices to ensure they continue to support your evolving values.

Maintaining an open and honest dialogue with your loved ones about your values and financial priorities is also crucial. You can make collective decisions that benefit the entire family by fostering a supportive environment where everyone's values are respected and considered. This collaborative approach to financial decision-making can strengthen relationships and create a shared sense of purpose and unity.

The journey toward financial freedom is not merely about accumulating wealth but also discovering what truly matters to you and aligning your spending choices accordingly. By embracing the principles of value spending, you can create a fulfilling, purpose-driven life while also building a strong foundation for lasting financial success.

As you progress along this path, remember that the ultimate goal is not to adhere to arbitrary societal expectations but to cultivate a life that reflects your deepest values and passions. By doing so, you can live a life of abundance, joy, and purpose, secure in the knowledge that every dollar you spend is an investment in what truly matters to you.

In the words of the renowned poet and philosopher Henry David Thoreau, "The price of anything is the amount of life you exchange for it." A practical application of this quote is to think of every purchase in terms of hours worked. For example, buying the latest gadget for $1,000 will cost you 50 hours of your work if you make $20 per hour. So effectively, more than a week of your life is exchanged for this gadget. When you run this purchase by your values and are very intentional with your spending, you will know if this is a true necessity or just nice to have.

By adopting the principles of value spending, you are choosing to exchange your life for experiences, relationships, and pursuits that bring you lasting happiness and fulfillment while cutting expenses that are wasteful and unnecessary.

As you continue this journey, take one intentional spending decision at a time, and build the life you truly desire, grounded in the values that matter most to you while eliminating drainages that hold you back from achieving financial success.

Don't take my word for it...

"I managed to achieve a reduction in debt by over $12,000 to date and increased my savings account from zero to $8,000. I have been able to reduce some of our monthly expenses and bills by switching companies and advocating for myself when negotiating fees and costs. Our cell phone bill alone resulted in a savings of $3,800. I gained confidence in myself. Also the change in mindset I have been able to grow. I truly feel and see my goals of being wealthy as a more attainable and achievable goal. I did not know before the correlation between mindset and wealth."

- Jessica H.

Very Next Action Steps

1. **Track your expenses and identify your core values:** Begin by tracking all your expenses to gain insight into your spending habits. At the same time, take the time to identify your top five core values,

which are the guiding principles in your life. Be intentional in this process and choose values that truly resonate with you.

2. **Evaluate your expenses based on your values:** Examine your expenses and compare them to your identified core values. Determine which expenses align with your values and which do not. Make a plan to eliminate or reduce expenses that don't support your values while prioritizing and investing in those that do.

Make a Difference

"We make a living by what we get, but we make a life by what we give."

- Winston Churchill

Isn't it amazing how a single act of kindness can ripple out and touch so many lives? It's like tossing a pebble into a pond and watching the ripples spread out, touching every corner. That's the power of giving, and today, I want to invite you to be a part of this beautiful ripple effect.

Imagine this:

There's someone out there right now, just like you were a few years ago. They're hungry for knowledge, eager to make a difference, and searching for a guiding light in the often-confusing world of money. They're standing at the edge of their own financial journey, ready to take that first step. But they need a little encouragement, a little guidance. And that's where you come in.

Our mission at Unshakable Wealth is to empower individuals with the tools they need to achieve financial success. But to do that, we need to get this book into the hands of those who need it most. If this book has sparked a new idea, lifted your spirits, or added any value to your life, I'm asking you, from the bottom of my heart, to take a moment right now to write an honest review. It will take you less than a minute.

Your review is like a beacon of light for someone else on their journey. It's a signpost that says, "This way to financial success," so they start taking control of their money and live a life of less financial fear and stress. It's a way for you to reach out and touch someone else's life without ever leaving your home.

What's even more magical is this: 90% of the profits from this book go straight to orphanages and kids in need, teaching them financial literacy. Your contribution, therefore, extends far beyond a single review — you are contributing to a cause that empowers the next generation with financial knowledge, and that's a priceless gift.

So, are you ready to create a ripple of change? It's as simple as leaving a review. Together, we can create a wave of financial empowerment that will touch lives for generations to come.

On Audible – click on the three dots in the top right of your device, then click "Rate & Review" and leave a few sentences about the book with a star rating.

On an e-reader or Kindle – the feature to leave a review will automatically come up when you scroll to the bottom of the book, then swipe up.

If the two options above didn't work, go to the Amazon book page or another place you bought the book and leave a review on the page.

And, to change even more lives, why not gift a copy of this book to someone you care about? It's like passing the torch of financial success to someone else and watching as they light up their own prosperous path.

Remember, your journey to financial prosperity it's about you and all the lives you touch along the way. So, let's start making waves.

From the bottom of my heart, thank you!

Your down-to-earth friend,

Lari

CHAPTER 5

The Super Savings Tactics

5.1 - Focus on Smart Savings and Uncover Hidden Opportunities

"Beware of little expenses; a small leak will sink a great ship." - Benjamin Franklin

It's too easy to become consumed by a scarcity mindset, constantly seeking ways to cut, reduce, and eliminate expenses. While being an extreme saver has its merits, it can also drive you into unnecessary worry and potentially hold you back from earning more. Instead, it's time to shift our focus to a more abundant mentality that centers around optimizing our spending plan, as mentioned in the previous chapter, supercharging our savings, and boosting wealth in a productive and meaningful way.

As you continue tracking your expenses, aligning them with your core values, and eliminating expenses that don't resonate with them, you're effectively capturing immediate savings and directing more of your hard-earned money back into your pocket rather than someone else's.

It's crucial to optimize your expenses further and identify areas where you can negotiate for additional savings and increased cash flow. For instance, consider the significant portion of your money that goes toward food. To save money in this category, you could plan your menu in advance, watch for sales, and utilize a credit card that offers cash back on grocery purchases. Of course, make sure you are wise with your credit card usage; pay it in full every month to avoid paying interest. By optimizing this expense, you can potentially save hundreds to thousands of dollars a year.

Now, let's explore the art of negotiation. You may wonder why large companies care about a single customer enough to offer discounts or negotiate rates. The simple answer is that customer retention is critical for their bottom line. Acquiring a new customer often costs more than retaining a loyal one, and maintaining a reputation for excellent customer service is essential to their success.

Consider the following list of bills that can be negotiated to potentially save hundreds or even thousands of dollars each year — funds that you can invest to accelerate your wealth-building process:

- **Credit card bills:** Negotiate lower interest rates, remove late and annual fees, or switch to a card with better rewards (such as travel rewards to save on trips or cash back).

- **Cable, satellite, or streaming services:** Discuss options for eliminating channels you don't watch or bundling services for a better deal, or cancel them altogether. I choose not to have cable and read more books to grow.

- **Phone bills and internet services:** Explore potential discounts or alternative plans that could save you money or switch to a different provider altogether. One of my students saved thousands of dollars and got additional perks with just a few phone calls.

- **Medical bills:** Inquire about possible discounts or payment plans to reduce your overall out-of-pocket costs. One time my older daughter had to go to the emergency room. There were some issues with the services they provided, and when the bills came, I asked for an itemized bill. After a few conversations, our bill was cut almost in half.

- **Insurance premiums:** Research and compare various providers to find the best rates or negotiate with your current provider for a better deal. I do this every year when my insurance is up for renewal, and every time, I have been able to save money and keep the same or better coverage.

It's crucial to be well-prepared with the right data to negotiate effectively. Start by reviewing your current insurance plans, cable, internet, and phone services to understand your coverage and costs. Print out the information or save it in a designated computer folder for easy access during negotiations. This way, you'll be able to maintain your coverage while working on reducing the costs.

Specifically, for insurance costs often overlooked due to auto-pay setups, do an online search, and find a reputable website to get free quotes for many insurance providers at once. I negotiate my home and car insurance yearly to save and invest more.

Once you've shopped around, it's time to start calling providers, including your current ones, to negotiate a better deal. You can follow the directions at the end of this section under resources to access the negotiating scripts to use during negotiation. When calling, remember to stay polite but firm. It's essential to be respectful and understand that the representative is an actual human doing their job, so don't get upset, as that won't result in any cooperation. Trust me, being kind and respectful goes a long way.

If you encounter an uncooperative representative, don't hesitate to call again and speak with someone else. Many people give up after the first call, but persistence can lead to significant savings.

Keep in mind that companies offer discounts to attract or retain high-value customers. Emphasize why you're a great customer, and you'll see results and uncover fantastic deals.

By adopting these strategic saving and negotiation tactics, you put more of your hard-earned money into your pocket and, ultimately, into your wealth-building machine.

Very Next Action Steps

1. **Research and gather data:** Review your current insurance, cable, internet, phone services, etc., to understand your coverage and costs. Print out or save the information in a designated folder for easy access during negotiations. Research alternative providers and compare quotes to find better deals.

2. **Negotiate with providers:** Call your service providers, including your current ones, to negotiate better deals using the negotiation scripts provided. Be polite but firm and emphasize your value as a customer. If you encounter an uncooperative representative, call again, and speak with someone else. Persistence can lead to significant savings.

Resources: Get the Scripts here: ***unshakablewealth.com/bookgifts***

5.2 - Design a Strategic Accounts Structure

"Discipline is the bridge between goals and accomplishment." - Jim Rohn

Creating the proper account structure is fundamental to achieving financial success and building wealth. With the proper accounts in place, you can strategically manage your finances to maximize your savings and ensure you're living with less financial stress and more smart money management. The account structure will align with the financial goals you have created during Phase One of this book. Let's dive deep into the types of accounts you should consider and understand how they contribute to your overall financial success in a way that will keep you more at peace and more financially confident.

The Emergency Fund

An emergency fund is vital for financial stability, providing a safety net for unexpected expenses and giving you peace of mind. Picture this: You suddenly lose your job, your car breaks down, or a medical emergency arises. This fund is designed to protect your cash flow during such emergencies, helping prevent financial stress in times of crisis. To effectively manage your emergency fund, you need to clearly understand your monthly expenses. This knowledge will allow you to set aside four months' worth of expenses in a High Yield Savings Account (HYSA).

Additionally, keep another two months' worth of expenses in cash and precious metal coins in a safe. This ensures you have access to funds in case of an IRS audit, identity theft, a lawsuit, or a natural disaster. Having a well-organized emergency fund is key to maintaining financial stability.

Long-Term Savings Goals

In addition to your emergency fund, you should have savings accounts designated for long-term goals, like a wedding, buying a home, or starting a business. Close your eyes and envision achieving these goals; this is what you're working toward. Label these accounts according to your specific objectives to stay motivated and focused. Consider using an HYSA that allows you to split your savings into multiple sub-accounts for various goals, making it easier to stay organized and on track.

The Wealthy Life Savings Account

This HYSA account is for guilt-free spending on short-term goals and indulgences, such as vacations or good-quality clothes. Start by allocating a small percentage of your take-home pay to this account and increase it if appropriate as your income grows. By setting aside funds for the things you enjoy, you can strike a balance between saving and living life to the fullest. Imagine sipping cocktails on a tropical beach or wearing that outfit you've always dreamed of — this account makes those dreams a reality.

Charitable Giving Account

Generosity is like a boomerang that finds its way back to you, so a charitable giving account should be part of your financial plan. By regularly contributing to this account, you can support causes that are in line with your values while experiencing the joy and fulfillment of giving. Imagine the smiles on the faces of those you're helping and the gratitude they feel — this account allows you to positively impact the world.

Checking Account

Your checking account is the central hub where your income flows in, and funds are distributed to your various savings accounts. Rather than going with big banks that charge you all kinds of fees, an interest-bearing, fee-free checking account, like an online checking account, is a great and more cost-effective alternative for this purpose. Think of it as the engine of your financial car, pumping energy into your other accounts and maintaining your financial health.

Wealth-Building Account

As you gain control over your finances, eliminate debt, and identify savings opportunities, the extra money you accumulate should go into a wealth-building account. Parkinson's law states that when your income increases, your expenses often rise to meet it. To avoid this trap, have a plan for allocating surplus funds to grow your wealth. Envision your financial future becoming brighter and more secure as you deposit funds into this account connected to retirement accounts and brokerage accounts to invest that money monthly and make your money work hard for you.

In the later chapters, we will discuss the money flow and percentages to allocate to each account. For now, focus on creating and organizing these accounts to establish a strong financial foundation.

Translating your goals into setting up a proper account structure is crucial for taking control of your finances and achieving your financial goals. By having separate accounts for emergency funds, long-term savings, short-term spending, charitable giving, and wealth-building, you can efficiently manage your money and enjoy life while building wealth. Remember, the ultimate goal is not to deprive yourself but to strike a balance between living a prosperous life and securing your financial future. By implementing this account structure, you're taking a significant step toward true financial freedom.

As you progress on your financial journey, remember to periodically review and adjust your account structure to accommodate your changing circumstances and goals. Life is filled with unexpected changes and detours, and your financial plan should be flexible enough to adapt to these changes.

Continue to educate yourself on personal finance, seek expert advice, and learn from the experiences of others who have walked the path to financial success.

In the end, creating the proper account structure is not just about managing your money; it's about creating a life that you can truly enjoy and be proud of without falling into the trap of lifestyle creep by spending more than you earn and investing a sizable chunk of your money to live a financially prosperous future. By taking these steps, you are securing your financial future and setting an example for future generations to follow.

Remember that every person's financial situation is unique, and the account structure presented here is a general guide. As you embark on your journey to financial confidence, customize your account structure to suit your specific needs and objectives. Embrace the process and take pride in your progress, knowing that with each step, you build a solid foundation for a lifetime of financial success and happiness.

Now that you've reached the end of this section, take a moment to reflect on what you've learned and how you can apply these concepts to your own financial life. Remember, the journey to financial success may not be smooth sailing, but the rewards are well worth the effort. Armed with the knowledge and tools outlined in this chapter, you're on your way to creating a better account structure for your hard-earned money.

Very Next Action Steps

1. **Assess and set up new accounts:** Analyze your current accounts, set up any missing ones (emergency, long-term savings, wealthy life savings, charitable giving, checking, and wealth-building), and customize them to align with your financial goals.

2. **Fund your emergency account:** Calculate your total monthly expenses, set aside four months' worth in a High Yield Savings Account, and store two months' worth in cash and precious metal coins in a safe.

5.3 - Automate Your Money with the "Pay Yourself First" Model

"Do not save what is left after spending, but spend what is left after saving." - Warren Buffett

Ah, the thrill of payday! You've worked hard, and it's time now to enjoy the fruits of your labor. Letting your imagination run wild with thoughts of shopping sprees, vacations, and memorable nights out is tempting. But before you begin to indulge, let's delve into a transformative concept that can help you achieve financial success in the long run: the "Pay Yourself First" model.

As a seeker of financial wisdom and prosperity, you want to learn about personal finance and grow your wealth over time. You might have heard the phrase "Pay Yourself First" in blogs or podcasts, but what does it really mean? It's a profound yet simple concept where you prioritize saving and investing a portion of your income before spending on anything else. This section will explore the benefits of the "Pay Yourself First" model and guide you through the steps to automate your money for long-term financial prosperity.

I recall my days in Moldova when I watched my mom struggle to make ends meet with the little money she had. And when my brother and I lived alone on only $133 a month for our expenses, we had to make tough choices and be incredibly frugal to stretch that money as far as possible. This conscious spending habit continued when I stayed in the U.S. with $20 in my pocket, through college, and even after I landed a high-paying job. These experiences taught me the importance of being mindful of my spending and the power of choice in determining my financial future.

Today, I want to share this life-transforming lesson with you. Using the "Pay Yourself First" model, you can take control of your finances to create a more prosperous life that reflects your deepest values and aspirations.

Before I dive into the specifics, I would like to share a quick story from my early days in the U.S. When I first arrived in Galveston, Texas, I had no idea how to navigate the complex world of American finance. I met a few mentors along my journey in the USA, like Elizabeth, Danny, John, & Suzanne, who became my guiding stars in this new land. They helped me adapt to the culture and grow into a better person and showed me the ropes of managing and investing money, including the value of paying yourself first, in America. Their support and encouragement were instrumental in my journey to financial success.

Let's embark on a transformative journey to automate your money with the "Pay Yourself First" model.

Step 1: Discover Your True Savings and Investment Goals

The first step to implementing the "Pay Yourself First" model is connecting with your savings and investment goals. Reflect on your deepest aspirations and consider your SMART goals for wealth and abundance in Chapter 2. How much money do you need to achieve these goals? Break them down into monthly or weekly targets to create a clear and inspiring roadmap for your financial future.

Remember to consider your emergency fund, retirement savings, and other long-term financial goals, like funding your children's education or buying a home. Having a vivid picture of your financial targets allows you to allocate your income more effectively and prioritize your future over immediate gratification.

Step 2: Embrace Your Unique "Pay Yourself First" Percentage

Once you clearly understand your financial goals, it's time to determine the percentage of your income you want to save and invest. This percentage will vary based on your individual circumstances and priorities. When I started to make money, I chose to save and invest at least 30% to 50% of my income. This helped me pay cash for my car, finance 60% of my bachelor's tuition to graduate debt-free and start investing.

I still vividly remember getting a call from the mortgage lender: "Congratulations! You got approved for $380,000 to buy your first house." I was in my twenties, and with the amount of money I got approved for, I knew that, at the time, it would buy me a 3000 sq. ft. home with a pool in the Houston, Texas, area. Being anchored in my values and staying committed to my financial freedom goals, I chose to buy a $165,000 house with low maintenance to make most of my money work for me through saving & investing.

If you're starting your financial journey or have a limited income, don't be discouraged if you can't save 30% immediately. Even small savings can accumulate significantly over time and help you develop a habit of prioritizing your financial future. As your income grows and your expenses go down through applying the spending optimization and saving principles discussed previously, you can gradually increase your "Pay Yourself First" percentage, embracing the power of incremental change and steadfast commitment to your goals.

Step 3: Transform Your Financial Life by Automating Your Savings and Investments

Automating your savings and investments is the key to successfully implementing the "Pay Yourself First" model. Setting up automatic transfers ensures that a portion of your income goes directly into your savings and investment accounts before you even have a chance to spend it. This eliminates the temptation to splurge on non-essential items and helps you stay on track to achieve your financial goals.

Here's how to transform your financial life through automation:

Set up direct deposit: If you haven't done so yet, arrange for your employer to deposit a portion of your paycheck into a company-sponsored retirement account such as 401k, IRA or other. Especially if there is an employer match benefit, this is like getting a raise and free money. Would you pass up free money? I hope not. Next, set up a direct deposit for your paycheck directly into your bank checking account. This way, your money will be available for immediate allocation to your various financial goals.

As mentioned before, *open separate high-yield savings and investment accounts:* To avoid commingling your funds and ensure you're allocating your money according to your financial goals. Open separate accounts for your emergency fund, other non-employer retirement savings, and investments. This will also make it easier to track your progress and make adjustments as needed.

Schedule automatic transfers: Set up recurring transfers from your checking account to your savings and investment accounts based on your "Pay Yourself First" percentage. You can do this monthly or bi-weekly, depending on your pay schedule.

Reassess and adjust: Periodically review your financial goals and your "Pay Yourself First" percentage. You may need to adjust your savings rate or reallocate your investments to stay on track as your financial circumstances change.

Step 4: Prioritize Your Expenses and Live a Life Aligned with Your Values

With your savings and investments automated, you can now focus on managing your remaining income to cover your essential expenses and discretionary spending. Create an optimized spending plan for necessities like housing, utilities, groceries, transportation, and discretionary items like entertainment, dining out, and shopping.

As previously discussed, unlike budgeting might feel like a stressful restrictive diet, an optimized value spending plan aligned with your values is a powerful tool that can help you gain control over your finances and get you closer to your financial goals while still enjoying life today. A well-crafted, optimized savings plan serves as a roadmap, guiding you through your spending decisions and ensuring you're allocating your resources intentionally to align with your priorities and values.

Let's explore a bit deeper how to create an optimized value spending plan:

1. **Track your income and expenses:** Before creating a plan, you need to know with certainty where your money is going and where it's coming from. And this is where the money tracking system we covered before comes into play. Track all your income sources, including your salary, side hustles, and any passive income streams. Make sure to keep track of all your expenses, including fixed costs such as rent or mortgage payments, utilities, and insurance, and variable expenses such as clothing, groceries, and entertainment.

2. **Categorize your expenses:** If you use an app, the expenses would already be grouped into categories, such as housing, transportation, food, entertainment, etc. If you use a spreadsheet, you would have to group them yourself. This will help you see the bigger picture of your spending habits and determine areas where you can cut back or reallocate funds.

3. **Set spending limits for each category:** Based on your income and financial goals, set a spending limit for each category of expenses. Be realistic and ensure your limits are achievable; starting with a more lenient spending plan and tightening it up over time is better than setting yourself up for failure with overly restrictive limits.

4. **Implement a system to track your spending:** Stay on top of your spending plan with the tracking system we previously covered to keep a pulse on your spending throughout the month.

5. **Adjust your optimized value spending plan as needed:** Your spending plan should be a living document that evolves with your financial circumstances and priorities. Regularly review your spending plan and make adjustments as needed, whether that means increasing your savings goals, cutting back on discretionary spending, or reallocating funds between categories.

You can make better financial decisions and avoid debt by prioritizing your expenses and living below your means. Remember that small sacrifices today can lead to significant rewards in the future. Embrace a life aligned with your values, where every financial decision is a conscious choice that brings you closer to your dreams.

In conclusion, the "Pay Yourself First" model is a powerful and transformative strategy for taking control of your finances and building long-term wealth. By automating your savings and investments, setting clear financial goals, and living a life aligned with your values, you will gain more financial confidence, unlocking the doors to a brighter, more abundant future.

Very Next Action Steps

1. **Determine and automate your "Pay Yourself First" percentage:** Reflect on your financial goals, determine the percentage of your income you want to save and invest and automate transfers from your checking account to your separate high-yield savings and investment accounts based on your "Pay Yourself First" percentage.

Resources: Get the Money Flow Autopilot Diagram here: ***unshakablewealth.com/bookgifts***

5.4- Get Paid What You Are Worth

"When you know your worth, no one can make you feel worthless." *– Anonymous*

You're here because you're ready for more, right? More wealth, more freedom, more choices. And let me tell you something you may not expect — you need more money to get there. It's not a shocking revelation. But how do you get there? How do you grow your wealth faster, seize those dreams and unlock financial freedom more quickly?

Well, one solid way is through a salary increase. I can almost hear your internal monologue saying, *A raise? Just like that?* Yes, exactly like that. You can negotiate a salary increase at your current job or explore new opportunities within or outside your current company. Landing a new job with a great salary outside your current company is a big topic with many important parts (resume, interviews, networking, etc.), so here we'll cover getting a raise at the current company.

First, create a folder in your work email. Name it "wins." Next, sift through your older emails. Look for and save any email where you've received positive feedback from colleagues, your boss, clients, customers — anyone from your work sphere. This isn't a time to be modest. If they've said something nice about your work, support, or collaboration skills, it goes in the "wins" folder. This will serve as a concrete testament to your value in the company, backing up your case for a salary increase.

Next, open a document — it could be on Word, Google Docs, or any other platform you're comfortable with. List all the tasks and projects you're currently working on. Each week, dedicate about 30 minutes to an hour updating this document with your achievements, even if they seem small or insignificant. Remember, in the grand scheme of things, the little wins add up. Jot down the departments you've worked with, your interactions, and any significant milestones you've reached. When you document your achievements, try to estimate the financial value or soft benefits they've brought to the company. For example, if you've automated a process or simplified a workflow, calculate the hours saved, and convert that into dollar terms. This will serve as a quantifiable measure of your contribution to the company.

The next step in your salary negotiation strategy involves a meeting with your boss. Schedule this meeting about six months or more before your performance review. In this meeting, convey your ambition to be a top performer and demonstrate your commitment by presenting the list of tasks and projects you're working on. Discuss your strengths, providing examples of your stellar performance and areas where you're still learning. Seek their opinion on the top three most valuable and meaningful accomplishments you could achieve within your projects that would elevate you to the top performer. Ensure your goals are achievable within the six months of your performance review. Once you have exceeded expectations and achieved these goals, indicate that you want to discuss a compensation adjustment.

After this meeting, put together an email summarizing the points discussed and send it to your boss. This serves as a written record of your conversation and sets a clear expectation for the future. Schedule weekly check-ins with your boss to discuss your progress and ensure you're on track.

Three weeks before your performance review, with your goals accomplished, it's time to marshal your support. Ask your colleagues to send emails acknowledging the positive impact of your work in achieving those goals. These endorsements and the accolades in your "wins" folder will serve as powerful testimonials when you sit down with your boss to discuss your salary raise.

Before this crucial meeting, do your homework. Research sites online to understand the market value for your role. This will help establish a fair salary expectation and strengthen your bargaining position. Enter the meeting prepared with this salary information, your list of accomplished goals, and the glowing testimonials from your "wins" folder. This, my friend, is your moment to shine. This is when you demonstrate your worth and advocate for the compensation you deserve.

And then, you've done it. You got the raise.

But what if you don't get the raise? Remember, not every battle is won, but they all teach us something. Ask for feedback on improving and making a better case next time. Alternatively, you may look for better growth opportunities elsewhere. You can leverage your accomplishments, data, and testimonials in your resume and interviews to negotiate a higher salary offer at another company. Following this process puts you in a win-win position.

As you navigate these steps, remember that building wealth it's about how much you save, invest, and earn. Getting paid what you're worth is crucial to mastering the art of a prosperous life. It's about respecting your work, your skills, and your contribution.

To get paid what you're worth, you must first believe you're worth it. You are.

And that wraps up our deep dive into the Super Savings Tactics. Next, we'll be shifting gears to discuss Achieving Compounding Growth. We'll explore the magic of compounding, how to calculate your Dream Life number, the secrets of stock market investing, and the power of passive real estate income.

Don't take my word for it...

"I was financially unstable, spending too much money every month and placing myself more in debt, $127,000 to be exact. I was able to save on a monthly basis $3,800. I was impressed by what I was able to accomplish, honestly thought that I would save just around $800 on a monthly basis but exceed my expectations by $3000. I was able to achieve great savings that I thought were not possible. I developed a willingness to go all in on myself, getting out of my comfort zone and applying for positions that I did not think I would get noticed for. Lari helped me land great interviews with various companies with an amazing resume she helped me create. This experience has really shown me that God works in mysterious ways."

- Saul R.

Very Next Steps

1. **Track Your Achievements:** Create a "wins" folder in your email and a document to track your work accomplishments and their value. Regularly update them with positive feedback and achievements.

2. **Discuss Your Goals with Your Boss:** Schedule a meeting with your boss. Present your work and set three achievable goals to elevate your performance.

3. **Prepare for Your Salary Negotiation:** Before your performance review, collect testimonials, research your role's market value, and prepare your case. If unsuccessful, use the feedback for future negotiations.

PHASE 3

Achieving Compounding Growth

"Compound interest is the eighth wonder of the world.
He who understands it, earns it. He who doesn't, pays it."
- Albert Einstein

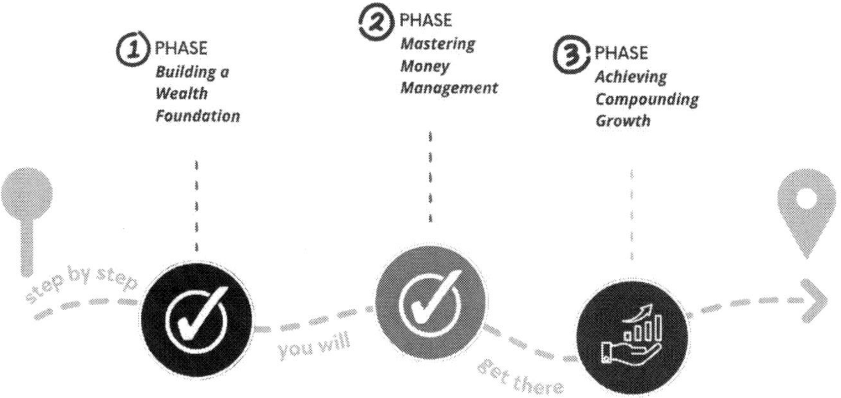

CHAPTER 6

The Ultimate Investing Secrets

6.1 - Calculate Your Dream Life Number

"If you can dream it, you can achieve it." - Zig Ziglar

You've worked hard to build a wealth foundation and master money management. Now it's time to dive into the world of investing. In this section, we'll explore how to calculate your Dream Life number to understand what you would need to achieve the life you've always wanted. After all, who doesn't dream of a life filled with freedom, security, and the ability to follow their passions?

Many talk about wanting to be wealthy, achieve financial freedom, and live a dream life. And only some ask themselves this question: *How much do I need to achieve financial freedom?* This is a question that I hope many will start thinking about and take action on. If you're anything like me, you've probably wondered about it too.

Here is the secret that only a few know. The right approach is to reverse engineer the path to financial freedom and answer the question: "How little do I need to achieve financial freedom by calculating my Dream Life (DL) number?" Your DL number is the amount of passive income needed to cover your daily living expenses. This income, generated from your savings and investments, would allow you to quit your job if you wanted to. It provides you the freedom and control to make decisions based on your passions and desires and live the life of your dreams.

Don't worry if calculations make you nervous; it's a simple formula, and we have a spreadsheet to help you. As mentioned earlier, each step of this path builds on the previous one. Now, you will bring your SMART goals, dream life vision board, and optimized current monthly expenses together. It's time to revisit what we covered before and set your savings and investing goals. We'll discuss three levels of dream life, which are unique to each person and what they value.

1. **Financial Security:** This level of the dream life is about having enough money to cover life's necessities while enjoying a sense of stability. Let's say your essential expenses amount to $4,000 a month. Multiply that by 12, and you'll need $48,000 of passive income annually. Using the Rule of 25, we can calculate your retirement savings, which is a cozy nest egg of $1.2 million. Remember, these are just starting points, and life can throw curveballs. You can save 30 times or more of your annual expenses if early retirement is on your radar.

2. **Financial Independence:** Welcome to the land where your money works for you, and you can maintain your current lifestyle without being tied to a 9-to-5 job. If your monthly expenses amount to $7,000, your Financial Independence (FI) number would be $2.1 million. But what if your dreams go beyond this? Perhaps you envision a mansion, globetrotting adventures, a vacation home, or a luxury car? In that case, it's time for:

3. **Financial Freedom:** At this stage, you're free from the daily grind and living life to the fullest with all the extras that make it even more amazing. To figure out your FF number, you'll need to research the

costs of your dream items like a house, car, boat, or vacation home and include luxury travel expenses like upscale hotels, exciting activities, and exotic locations. This will give you a realistic goal for your financial freedom lifestyle and the investment needed to reach it.

Now that you've calculated your Dream Life number, it's time to build on your game plan to make it happen. Continue reviewing & refining your current financial situation and identifying areas where you can optimize expenses, increase savings, and invest smarter.

Next, define a realistic timeline for achieving your goals.

Understand that everyone's financial journey is unique, and being patient and persistent is essential. Maintaining a growth mindset and continually educating yourself about personal finance and investing is vital. Stay informed about market trends, new investment opportunities, and tax laws that may affect your financial plan. Moreover, be open to adjusting your approach as your life circumstances change or as new information becomes available.

Very Next Action Steps

1. **Calculate your Dream Life number:** Determine the level of financial security, independence, or freedom you desire, and calculate the passive income needed to cover your living expenses.

2. **Refine your financial plan:** Review and optimize your current financial situation, identifying areas to reduce expenses, increase savings, and invest smarter.

3. **Set a realistic timeline and maintain a growth mindset:** Establish a realistic timeline for achieving your goals, continuously educate yourself about personal finance and investing, and stay open to adjusting your approach as needed.

Resource: Get the Free Dream Life number spreadsheet here: ***unshakablewealth.com/bookgifts***

6.2 - Demystifying Investing and Its Potential

"It's not about being rich to invest, and it's not about timing the market. It's about being in the market starting as early as possible." - Larisa Olteanu

What is investing?

Investing is when you use your money to buy things that can grow in value. The goal is to make more money than what you started with. When you invest, you're trying to make your money work hard for you, not only when you are asleep but 24 hours a day, seven days a week, 365 days a year. Investing is like planting seeds in a garden to grow more food later. Instead of seeds, you use your money to buy assets with the goal of making more money in the future. However, there is always a chance that things might turn out differently than expected, just like sometimes seeds don't grow, or the crops get affected by the weather or other conditions. But if you choose wisely and learn about what you're investing in, it could help you save money and achieve your financial freedom goals. There are many investment products to choose from. Whatever you choose to invest in, you hope it will be successful and pay you back with even more money.

Is investing risky?

Investing is risky and has the probability of losing some or all of the money that was initially invested. However, you must understand that nothing in this life is without risk. Every day we are exposed to some type of risk. The question is how much or how little risk we are willing to take. In the financial world, this is called risk tolerance.

Let's look at a person who chooses to drive a car and a person that loves riding a motorcycle. Both are at risk of getting in an accident at any moment. However, the person riding a motorcycle has a significantly greater chase of severe injury than the person in the car. Therefore, the car driver takes less risk than the motorcycle rider.

Here is another example, some people love rock climbing, while others will stick to a walk in the park. Either one of these people can trip and fall, breaking their bones, but the risk that the rock climber is taking is much greater than a walk in the park. The point is everything carries a risk in life, including how you choose to invest your money.

In the financial world, there is a relationship between the amount of risk taken and the returns one will get. Investors try to lower their risk and protect themselves from losing money by putting money into different investments. This is called diversification which helps spread the risk, similar to not putting all your eggs in one basket, with the hope that if one asset is not performing, the others will pull the weight. Investing small amounts of money over a long time is a good idea. This can help you avoid investing all your money at the wrong time.

There are many investments to consider and choose from, and you must consider all your options carefully and determine which diversification strategy makes sense for you. Diversification can help you reduce risk, but it's not a guarantee that you won't lose money.

There are two very important concepts we will cover that are tied to risk: Asset allocation and asset diversification.

1. **Asset allocation:** A strategy investors use to decide how to divide their money among different asset classes, such as real estate, paper assets (e.g., stocks, bonds, etc.), cash, commodities, etc.

   Think of it like deciding how to divide a pie among different people. The investor decides how much money they want to put into each type of investment based on their goals, risk tolerance, and market conditions.

   The idea behind asset allocation is to strike a balance between risk and reward by creating an investment portfolio. There are different levels of risk depending on types of investments and return, so by spreading money across different types of assets, investors can reduce the risk of losing all their money in one type of investment.

   Asset allocation is an important part of any investment strategy, and it should be periodically reviewed and adjusted based on changes in the investor's goals or market conditions.

2. **Asset diversification:** A strategy investors use to spread their money across different types of investments within a particular asset class. For example, in real estate, that might look like investing in residential real estate, apartments, storage units, etc. For the paper asset class, stocks, bonds, etc.

   Think of it like *not* putting all your eggs in one basket. By investing in various stocks or bonds, investors can reduce their exposure to the risk of any company or bond issuer.

For example, if an investor only invests in one stock and that company experiences financial trouble, the investor could lose a lot of money. However, if the investor diversifies their portfolio by investing in several different stocks, the impact of any one company's financial trouble is reduced.

Remember, it's important to know that asset allocation and diversification don't guarantee that an investor will not lose money.

Why invest?

I was at a grocery store the other day, and they had a lot of sampling tables. Behind those tables, 90% of the time were older people, and some were very old. This particular gentleman was serving samples of salty caramel popcorn; he was so fragile, and his legs were shaking from standing up. Finally, another employee got him a chair to sit down on. Seeing these older adults, especially knowing they were standing there for hours, broke my heart. No one should get to that age and go through that. You should not get to that age and suffer like that.

Many people face financial difficulties when they get older because they didn't learn about saving and investing and the power of compounding interest.

Let's explore some of the reasons why investing is essential:

1. **Inflation:** Picture the cost of a candy bar today compared to its price ten years ago. That difference is due to inflation — the small price increases of goods and services over the years. As prices rise, your money's value declines, meaning you can't buy as much with the same amount of cash. Stashing money in a traditional savings account erodes the value of money due to inflation. To counteract this, invest in assets that yield returns exceeding the inflation rate, thereby preserving, and growing your money.

For instance, imagine having $1,000 today with an annual inflation rate of 3%. In a year, your $1,000 will only buy what $970 could purchase today. However, investing that money with an 8% annual return will leave you with $1,080, outpacing inflation and maintaining your purchasing power.

2. **Building wealth:** You can't just save your way to retirement. Investing is a potent wealth-building tool, allowing you to harness the power of compounding interest over the long term. This effect is magnified when you invest regularly and remain disciplined.

   Think of a small stream that starts high up in the mountains. As it flows downhill, it is joined by other streams, eventually forming a mighty river. Similarly, investing lets your money compound and expand, resulting in a more significant sum over time. Assuming Vanguard data[3] from 1926 through 2021, we know that 60% of stocks and 40% of bonds portfolio had a return of 9.9%. By consistently investing $1,000 a month for 40 years, with an average annual return of 9.9%, you could accumulate more than $5.4 million, not accounting for fees which we will cover in more detail later. Such growth is only possible through investing.

3. **Financial security and independence:** Wise investing helps you establish a nest egg that provides financial security, independence, or freedom for you and your loved ones. A diversified investment portfolio could enable you to weather financial storms, such as job loss or unforeseen expenses, without resorting to debt.

   Moreover, investing assists in achieving financial goals like funding your children's education or enjoying a comfortable retirement. You must start investing sooner than later so there is more time for your

---

[3] https://investor.vanguard.com/investor-resources-education/education/model-portfolio-allocation

money to grow, preparing you better for these milestones. The key is not to time the market but be in the market as early as possible.

4. **Leaving a legacy:** Investing doesn't just create wealth for you; it also benefits future generations. By constructing a robust financial foundation, you can improve your children's and future grandchildren's lives, leaving a lasting legacy.

   Consider two families: one that invests and accumulates wealth over generations and another that spends all its income without saving or investing. The first family can provide their children with better education, healthcare, and opportunities, while the second family might struggle to make ends meet.

What is compounding interest?

If you have $1,000 and it earns 10% interest each year, at the end of the first year, you'll have $1,100. And, at the end of the second year, you'll have $1210. Not only did you earn $100 on the $1,000 you initially deposited — your original "principal" — but you also earned an extra $10 on the $100 in interest. Ten dollars may not seem like an amount that would make a difference, but it adds up over time. Even if you decide never to add more money to that account, in ten years, due to the power of compound interest, you'll have more than $2,593, and in 25 years, you'll have almost $10,834.

Let's look at compound interest from another angle. How much does an ice cream cost? Would you believe nearly $47,000? If an ice cream costs $5, and you buy it every week until you're old enough to retire, you'll spend $7,800 on ice cream. If you give up that ice cream and invest the money instead, earning 10% interest compounded every year for 30 years, you'll have more than $47,045.

Another important money rule to learn is the Rule of 72.

The Rule of 72 is a simple formula to approximate how long it will take for your investment to double in value at a given rate of return. So, if we assume a rate of return of 8%, take 72 and divide it by 8, which equals 9. This means your investment will double in value approximately every nine years. Understanding this simple rule will allow you to quickly estimate your investment's future value.

For example, if you invest $20,000 today, what would your investment be worth in 36 years? Let's assume the rate of return is 8%. Then in 9 years, the investment will double to $40,000. In 18 years, it will be $80,000. In 27 years, it would be $160,000, and in 36 years would be $320,000.

Let's cover the 4% rule.

The 4% rule is a guideline for retirees to determine how much they can safely withdraw from their retirement savings each year to fund their living expenses without running out of money. The rule states that, in the first year of retirement, retirees can withdraw 4% of their initial retirement portfolio balance and adjust that amount for inflation each subsequent year.

For example, if a retiree has a portfolio balance of $1 million, they could withdraw $40,000 in the first year they retire. Assuming the inflation rate is 2% the following year, the retiree will adjust their withdrawal amount to $40,800 (i.e., $40,000 x 1.02). The retiree would continue to adjust their withdrawal amount for inflation each year.

The 4% rule is based on historical market returns. However, there is no guarantee that the rule will work for every retiree, as market conditions and individual circumstances can vary. Retirees must review their retirement plans regularly to ensure they have enough income to support their needs throughout retirement.

What can you invest in?

The most important investment of all is yourself — this is your number one priority. My mom used to say, "They can take everything away from you, but no one will ever be able to take away your brain." If you lose everything, you will have your acquired knowledge, gained experience, network, and mastered skills to build things back up again.

My great-grandfather Vasile and I were watching the snow fall through the window while the moonlight was beautifully shining on the white ground. During those cold winter days, I loved listening to my great-grandfather telling stories about his life. This late-evening story was about money.

Vasile: "In my young days, your great-grandmother and I saved money in our attic between the hay stashes. And when our country Moldova became part of the Soviet Union in the 1940s, our currency was worth nothing, so we lost everything. Luckily, we had land and workers to help with our farming, which helped us survive. With the Soviet Union, things started to get more stable, and we had the opportunity to save money in a special savings account. For over 40 years, we saved a very large amount of money, but in 1989 the Soviet Union fell apart. The currency once again was worth nothing, not even good for toilet paper, so we lost everything we saved for so many years. Our farming skills and knowledge and our land saved us again."

The lesson that I learned that night from him was twofold. First, the skills and knowledge they gained helped them not only survive but also build a very sizable fortune after the first currency collapse. Second, owning tangible assets like land or other real estate is a smart choice compared to saving paper money in the bank that can be worth nothing one day.

If you take all the money in the world and give it to everyone equally, after a certain amount of time, the majority of the wealthy will return to being wealthy, and the majority of the poor will go back to being poor. Why?

Because of the acquired knowledge, gained experience, network, and mastered skills. Here are a few names of wealthy people, regardless of how you feel about them, who lost everything and returned to build their wealth again: Kim Basinger, Walt Disney, and Maggie Magerko.

Aside from investing in yourself, there are also these investment options:

1. **Your own business:** To do what you love, personal growth, for no limit on how much money you can make & tax advantages

2. **Real Estate:** Residential properties, apartments, storage units, shopping centers, land, etc.

3. **Paper Assets:** Stocks, bonds, mutual funds, index funds, ETFs. Etc.

4. **Commodities:** Commodities are physical goods like gold, silver, oil, or agricultural products that can be bought and sold on commodity exchanges.

5. **Other businesses & start-ups**

When it comes to paper assets, whether you decide to invest on your own or seek a professional, you must understand these key things:

1. You need to get financially literate about how the stock market works because if you don't, how would you know that the professional you hired is doing a great job?

2. If you hire a professional, understand the fees because those fees could eat up a huge chunk of your investments.

3. No one should invest in things that they don't understand. You need to learn how the stock market, real estate, or other investment vehicles work!

We discussed fees, so let's dive deeper into them and understand if they matter.

Like any purchase, investment products and services come with fees and expenses. Although these charges may appear insignificant, they can accumulate and massively impact your investment portfolio in the long term. Understanding the fees you pay to make informed investment decisions with your hard-earned money is crucial.

Once again, assuming Vanguard data[4] from 1926 through 2021, we know that 60% of stocks & 40% of bonds portfolio had a return of 9.9%. Here is an illustration of an investment portfolio with a 9.9% annual return over 40 years with three different ongoing fees of 0.3%, 1%, or 2%.

Annual investment fee	**0.30%**	**1%**	**2%**
Starting amount	$0	$0	$0
Years	40 years	40 years	40 years
Additional contributions	$1,000 per month, at the beginning of the month	$1,000 per month, at the beginning of the month	$1,000 per month, at the beginning of the month
Annualized rate of return	9.90%	9.90%	9.90%
Annual return after fees	9.60%	8.90%	7.90%
Total amount you will have contributed	$480,000.00	$480,000.00	$480,000.00
Total at the end of investment	**$5,009,586.53**	**$4,135,305.18**	**$3,156,057.09**

[4] https://investor.vanguard.com/investor-resources-education/education/model-portfolio-allocation

Taking the $5.4 million portfolio growth calculated before when investing in funds with ongoing fees of 0.3%, the cost to us, the investors, is about $432,000. At 1% fees, the cost is over $1.3 million — three times more! And, at 2% fees, the cost is almost $2.3 million, almost six times more than the 0.3% fees!! The 2% fees cost us almost 43% of our nest egg retirement portfolio!!!

But wait, there's more. This didn't account for the money manager/advisor investing our money in actively managed funds that could add another 1% on top of the 2%. Bringing the fees over $3 million and our nest egg retirement portfolio to $2,421,109, costing us almost 56% of our nest egg retirement portfolio, which is more than we have paid in fees rather than enjoying it in our retirement or living it as generational wealth to our loved ones.

When I first learned this, it completely blew my mind!!!

And 40 years doesn't account for an additional 25 years for the money managers/financial advisors to actively manage the investment portfolio post-retirement. So, over 65 years, the impact is astronomical.

Fees absolutely matter!

What about performance? Don't higher fees mean higher returns?

This study, published in 2020 by S&P Global, concluded that actively managed funds underperformed over ten years. "Large-cap funds made it a clean sweep for the decade. For the 10th consecutive one-year period, the majority (71%) underperformed the S&P 500."[5] And, when it comes to mid and small-cap, hang tight if you don't know what these names are just yet,

---

[5] https://www.spglobal.com/en/research-insights/articles/spiva-u-s-year-end-2019-scorecard-active-funds-continued-to-lag

"84% of mid-cap funds and 89% of small-cap funds underperformed over the longer 10-year period."[6] So, the "experts" are not beating the market.

It's your choice to hire a professional or invest on your own. If you choose to invest on your own, do your research and don't buy solely on stock tips from others; do your due diligence and research.

When it comes to fees, these are some great questions from investor.gov to ask yourself:

- What are the total fees to purchase, maintain, and sell this investment?
- Are there ways that I can reduce or avoid some of the fees I'll pay, such as by purchasing the investment directly?
- How much will this investment increase in value before I break even?
- What are the ongoing fees to maintain my account?

For mutual funds: How much will the fund charge me when I buy and/or sell shares?"[7]

If you choose to go with an investment professional, then ask them these questions:

- "How do you get paid? By commission? By the number of assets you manage? By another method?"
- "Do I have any choice on how to pay you?"
- Should I pay you by the transaction or pay a flat fee regardless of how many transactions I have?"[8]

---

[6] https://www.spglobal.com/en/research-insights/articles/spiva-u-s-year-end-2019-scorecard-active-funds-continued-to-lag
[7] https://www.investor.gov/introduction-investing/getting-started/understanding-fees
[8] https://www.investor.gov/introduction-investing/getting-started/understanding-fees

Want to know more about fees?

Here are a couple of types of fees that are a good start, but there are more:

- **Advisory fees:** If you work with a financial advisor, you can ask them about the fees associated with your investments. Advisors should be able to explain what costs you're paying and why. You can also find these on your account statements.

- **Expense ratios:** These fees are related to the actual investment, such as Mutual Funds, Index Funds, etc. The expense ratio is a percentage that shows how much of the fund's total assets are spent on administrative and other operating costs. For example, a fund might have an expense ratio of 0.3%. This means that 0.3% of the fund's total assets will be spent on yearly expenses.

So, now that you understand fees, performance, compounding, and becoming more financially literate about investing, it's time to learn more about the stock market.

Very Next Action Steps

1. **Assess your risk tolerance and financial goals:** Before you invest, evaluate your financial situation, goals, and risk tolerance. Consider your time horizon, liquidity need, and ability to withstand market fluctuations.

6.3 - Learn The Stock Market Investing

"The stock market is a device for transferring money from the impatient to the patient." - Warren Buffett

What are paper assets?

These assets are called paper assets because their ownership and value are documented on paper or electronically rather than having a physical form. Such assets include stocks, currencies, bonds, mutual funds, insurance plans, etc. Paper assets carry different levels of risk and return, and investors need to research and understand their investments before making any decisions.

What are stocks?

When a company wants to start or grow a business, it needs money. But sometimes it's not easy for a company to get all the money it needs from just one person or a bank. So, the company breaks up its ownership into little pieces called "shares." And the company starts selling those shares to the public.

If you own a share, you own a little piece of the company. And if the company does well, the value of your share goes up. But if the company doesn't do well, the value of your share goes down.

People can buy and sell a company's shares on the stock market. The stock market is where you, I, and others can buy and sell shares of different companies.

So, when you hear people talking about stocks, they usually talk about buying and selling company shares on the stock market. It's like buying and selling little pieces of ownership in a company.

Here are some reasons why some investments make money:

- If a company is growing and doing well, it can make more money and attract more people who want to buy its stocks. This can cause the stock price to go up.
- Companies sometimes share some of their profits with those who own their stocks. This is called a dividend, which can give investors some extra money.
- Some types of businesses or industries are more popular than others, and stocks from those industries might do well because more people want to buy them.
- If people hear good things about a company or its stock, they might want to buy it, which can increase the stock price.
- Sometimes, how the economy is doing can affect how well stocks do. If the economy is doing well, some stocks might do well too.
- Some companies have something special, like a unique product or proprietary technology, or some other advantage that makes them better than their competitors. This can make them more profitable and make investors want to buy their stocks.
- If the people in charge of a company are really good at their job, it can make investors feel good about buying their stocks.
- Sometimes, two companies join, or one company buys another. If investors think this will benefit the company, they might want to buy its stocks.

Here are some reasons why some investments don't make money:

- Sometimes, the company investors bought stocks in is not making enough money or is losing money, which can cause the stock price to drop.
- If the economy is not doing well, some stocks might not do well either.

- If a company has a lot of competition, it might not be able to make as much money, which can cause the stock price to go down.
- If the people in charge of the company make bad decisions.
- If a company has legal problems, like being sued or getting in trouble with the government.
- Sometimes, new things become popular and change the way businesses work.
- If a stock costs too much compared to how much money the company makes, people might sell it, which can cause the stock price to go down.
- Sometimes, things happen that nobody can predict, like a natural disaster or big political changes, which can cause stock prices to go down.
- If people hear bad things about a company or stock, they might not want to buy it, which can cause the stock price to go down.

There are two main types of stocks:

Common Stocks: These stocks represent ownership in a company and give shareholders the right to vote on certain company decisions at shareholder meetings. Common stockholders may also get dividends, which are a portion of the company's profits paid out to shareholders. If the company is successful, the value of the common stock may increase, allowing investors to sell their shares for a profit.

Preferred Stocks: These stocks give shareholders a priority claim on a company's earnings and assets over common stockholders. Preferred stockholders usually get fixed dividends which are paid out before the common stockholders get their dividends paid out. If the company goes under or needs to sell off its assets, preferred shareholders get paid before common shareholders. But, typically, preferred shareholders don't get to vote.

There are also different categories of stocks based on the size and characteristics of the companies, such as:

Large-cap stocks: These are stocks of companies with a large market capitalization, or the total value of all outstanding shares, usually over $10 billion.

Mid-cap stocks: These are stocks of companies with a medium market capitalization, usually between $2 billion and $10 billion.

Small-cap stocks: These are stocks of companies with a small market capitalization, usually under $2 billion.

International: Stocks of companies in other countries.

Growth stocks: Stocks of companies that may grow higher than other stocks or the overall market.

Value stocks: Stocks of companies that seem undervalued by the market and have a lower price-to-earnings ratio compared to the overall market.

What are bonds?

Bonds are a special way to lend money to a company or government.

Sometimes, companies, governments, or municipalities need money and give people the opportunity to buy bonds from them. When people buy bonds, they give the company or government the money they need. Then, the company or government promises to give the people their money back with interest after a certain amount of time.

Bonds can have different time limits, from a short time to a really long time. They can also be more or less risky, depending on how trustworthy the company or government is. The more trustworthy they are, the less extra money they have to pay back.

There are different types of bonds available, like corporate bonds, government bonds, municipal bonds, short-term bonds, long-term bonds, TIPS, etc.

What's the difference between stocks and bonds?

Let's say you would like to invest in a company that makes cookies but don't have enough money to start your own cookie business. Therefore, you are thinking of investing in a company that already makes and sells cookies. You have done thorough research and are convinced this is a solid company. There are two options: buying stocks or buying bonds.

If you decide to buy stocks, you will become a part owner of the cookie company. You would buy shares of the company's stock, and if the company does well and makes a profit, you could earn money in two ways: the value of the stock could go up, and the company may pay you a portion of its profits as dividends. However, if the company does poorly, the value of your stock could go down, and you may lose money.

If you decide to buy bonds, you will lend money to the cookie company. The company would pay you interest on the money you loaned them, and after a certain amount of time, they would pay you back the entire amount you loaned them. The bond usually has a fixed interest rate, so you know how much you will earn. If the company goes bankrupt, it might be unable to honor its promise of paying you back.

What are mutual funds?

A mutual fund is an investment that packages together many types of investments. Think of it as a big pot of money run by money managers or "investment advisors." These money managers make investment decisions on behalf of the fund's investors. The managers research and choose investments based on the fund's investment objectives.

Some mutual funds might be very narrow and contain only stocks. Others add bonds and other investments.

When investing in a mutual fund, people are buying a share of the fund's portfolio. If the fund's value goes up, the shares go up too. If the value goes down, the shares go down.

Think of a mutual fund like a big pot of soup at a community dinner. Everyone who contributes money to the pot gets a portion of the soup (the portfolio). The more money you put in, the bigger your portion.

Now, imagine the soup is made of various ingredients representing different investments. Some ingredients might be high-quality and expensive (like stocks of well-performing companies), while others might be more affordable and stable (like bonds or cash).

Over time, as the soup cooks, the flavors blend and change. If the expensive ingredients perform well (maybe the carrots and onions bring out a great flavor), the overall soup becomes tastier, and everyone's portion is worth more. However, if some ingredients don't perform well (let's say the potatoes are undercooked), the overall taste of the soup might suffer, and everyone's portion becomes less appetizing or valuable.

Like with the soup, when you invest in a mutual fund, you share the gains and losses of the fund's portfolio. The goal is to have more good "ingredients" perform well so that everyone's portion increases in value.

Mutual funds offer investors diversification, which means that by investing in a single mutual fund, investors might get exposure to various securities across many different companies and industries.

When investors buy or sell their shares in a fund, they might pay fees. These fees contribute to covering the costs and wages of those who manage the fund.

Fees charged when buying or selling mutual fund shares can accumulate over time and significantly reduce the returns that investors may receive. It's crucial to be aware of the costs of a mutual fund and how they may impact returns over the duration of time that you plan to hold the shares. If two mutual funds are similar in all other ways but have different fees, choosing the fund with lower fees will likely result in making more money.

What are index funds?

An index fund is a group of stocks trying to match a specific market index, like the Standard & Poor's 500, the Russell 3000, or the Wilshire 5000. Unlike traditional managed mutual funds, which rely on a team of managers to choose individual stocks, index funds use computer programs to buy and sell stocks to match the index holdings. Because index funds don't require active management, they generally have lower fees than managed funds. The return on investment is similar to the index minus any fees the fund charges.

Index funds are like baskets of different things that people can buy a piece of. These baskets hold stocks or bonds or other things, which are like small pieces of ownership in companies or debt.

Think of an index fund as a music playlist that mirrors the top charts. Let's say you want to listen to the most popular songs at the moment. Instead of individually selecting each song and adding it to your playlist, you could use a pre-made playlist that includes all the current top songs.

In this analogy, each song in the playlist represents a different stock in the market. The playlist as a whole represents the index fund. Just as the playlist automatically updates to reflect the current popular songs, an index fund automatically includes the companies in the index it's tracking. An example is a broad index like the S&P 500, which represents 500 of the largest U.S. companies.

The value of your playlist (index fund) goes up and down based on the popularity (stock price) of the songs (stocks) it includes. If most of the songs are hits, your playlist is highly valued. If many songs lose popularity, the value of your playlist decreases.

So, buying a share of an index fund, it's like enjoying a playlist of the market's top hits. You get a wide variety of songs (diversification) without the effort of picking each song individually (low management effort). However, the quality of your playlist (return on investment) ultimately depends on the performance of the individual songs (stocks).

Here is what wealthy people say about index funds:

"Index funds eliminate the risks of individual stocks, market sectors, and manager selection. Only stock market risk remains." - John C. Bogle.[9]

"A low-cost index fund is the most sensible equity investment for the great majority of investors. My mentor, Ben Graham, took this position many years ago, and everything I have seen since convinces me of its truth." - Warren Buffett.[10]

What are ETFs?

ETFs, or Exchange-Traded Funds, are investment funds. ETFs pool together investors' money to buy a portfolio of assets like stocks, bonds, etc.

Similar to index funds, ETFs track a specific market index, sector, or asset class. For example, an ETF focused on the S&P 500 holds a group of stocks

---

[9] Bogle, J. C. (2007). The Little Book of Common Sense Investing

[10] Bogle, J. C. (2007). The Little Book of Common Sense Investing

mirroring the S&P 500 index. When you buy an ETF, you are buying a share of the underlying assets held by the ETF.

ETFs have become more popular because of their low costs, diversification benefits, and liquidity. They are a convenient way for investors to gain exposure to different markets and asset classes without buying individual stocks or bonds. ETFs also allow investors to trade throughout the day at market-determined prices, unlike mutual funds, which are priced when the trading day ends.

What is a Target-Date Fund?

A target-date fund, also known as a lifecycle fund, allocates its investments among stocks, bonds, and other assets, with the investment mix determined by the investor's anticipated retirement date. The idea is that the asset allocation will automatically be adjusted over time into a more conservative one as the target date approaches.

For example, if an investor plans to retire in 2050, they could invest in a target-date fund with a target date of 2050. The fund will contain a more aggressive mix of stocks, bonds, and other assets that is appropriate for the age of the investor. As the target date approaches, the fund will gradually shift the asset allocation to a more conservative one as the person gets older.

Target-date funds are designed to be easy to understand and require very little maintenance.

However, it is important to note that target-date funds are not a one-size-fits-all solution. Different target-date funds may have different asset allocations, fees, and performance histories. Investors should carefully research and compare different options before choosing a target-date fund. Additionally, target-date funds are not immune to market fluctuations and can still lose value, so investors should always be prepared for potential risks.

What are REITs?

Real Estate Investment Trusts own and manage real estate properties that generate income. These properties can range from office buildings, shopping centers, apartment buildings, warehouses, and even hotels.

With REITs, individual investors can invest in real estate assets without having to directly buy, manage, or finance properties themselves. One can buy publicly traded REIT shares, which invest in real estate properties and generate income from rent, capital appreciation, and other means.

By law, REITs must distribute at least 90% of their taxable earnings to shareholders as dividends.

There are several REIT categories, including those focused on property ownership (equity REITs), those providing property financing (mortgage REITs), and those that combine both approaches (hybrid REITs).

Like any investment, REITs come with risks, including interest rate risk, market risk, and specific risks related to the underlying properties. Doing your own research and/or consulting with a professional before investing in REITs or any other investment is crucial.

What are investment portfolios?

A portfolio is a collection of assets like stocks, bonds, commodities, currencies, cash equivalents, and investment funds like mutual funds, ETFs, etc.

These assets are held directly by those that manage their own investments and/or are managed by financial professionals and investment managers. The purpose of a portfolio is to diversify the risk (spread it around) and increase the potential for returns.

Just like an artist's portfolio showcases a variety of their works, a financial portfolio demonstrates the range and diversity of an individual's or institution's investments. The specific composition of a portfolio depends on various factors, including the investor's investment goals, risk tolerance, financial situation, and time horizon.

Imagine standing at a buffet with all types of dishes, each representing a unique investment opportunity. The trick is to fill your plate with the right mix that suits your taste and nutritional needs. This is similar to crafting your investment portfolio. Below we will cover two well-known investment portfolios designed by financial experts Ray Dalio and David Swensen.

1. **Ray Dalio's All Weather Portfolio:** Ray Dalio, the founder of the investment firm Bridgewater Associates, developed a portfolio strategy known as the "All Weather Portfolio." This strategy aims to deliver consistent returns in any market environment, hence the name "all weather." Dalio's "All Weather Portfolio" allocation is as follows:

    30% Stocks
    40% Long-Term Bonds
    15% Intermediate-Term Bonds
    7.5% Gold
    7.5% Commodities

    According to Dalio, this balanced approach can help investors achieve their financial goals with less risk of significant losses, particularly during economic downturns. When building a portfolio, individual investors like you and I should carefully consider our own risk tolerance, investment goals, and time horizon before implementing this or any other strategy.

2. **David Swensen's Portfolio**[11]**:** David Swensen was the long-time chief investment officer at Yale University, overseeing the Yale Endowment. In his book, *Unconventional Success: A Fundamental Approach to Personal Investment*, Swensen proposed a portfolio for individual investors focusing on diversification and low-cost index funds. Here's the basic allocation he recommended:

    30% Domestic Stock Funds

    20% Real Estate Investment Trusts (REITs)

    15% U.S. Treasury Bonds

    15% Developed (Foreign) Market Stock Funds

    5% Emerging Market Stock Funds

    Swensen believes that this mix would provide a solid return while protecting against the ups and downs of the market. Like with Dalio's All Weather Portfolio, we should understand our own financial situation and goals before implementing this strategy.

Remember, it's crucial to do your own research to understand the potential risks and returns of these or any investment strategies. While these portfolio models provide a guide, they may not be suitable for everyone. Investing always involves risk, including the risk of loss.

How do you determine what to invest in?

Determining what to invest in depends on several factors, including your financial goals, risk tolerance, investment horizon, and personal interests. It's essential to create a well-rounded investment strategy that aligns with your financial objectives and risk profile. Here are some steps to help you decide what to invest in:

---

[11] David F. Swensen. (2005). Unconventional Success: A Fundamental Approach to Personal Investment.

Assess your financial goals: Start by reviewing your short-term and long-term SMART goals, such as setting money aside for a down payment on a house, children's education, financial freedom, retirement planning, etc. Knowing your goals will help you choose investments that align with your desired outcomes.

Determine your risk tolerance: Risk tolerance is your ability and willingness to accept potential losses in pursuit of higher returns. It's different for each person and is influenced by factors like age, income, and financial situation. Understanding your risk tolerance will help you select investments that suit your comfort level with volatility.

Establish your investment horizon: Your investment horizon refers to the amount of time you hold your investments before you need to use the money. A longer investment horizon generally allows for greater risk-taking, as you have more time to recover from potential losses. Choose investments with an appropriate time horizon based on your goals.

Diversify: Diversifying your portfolio is very important when it comes to investing. It's the ability to strategically spread your investments across various asset classes, industries, and geographical locations. This helps reduce risk and increase potential returns. Some common asset classes include stocks, bonds, real estate, and cash equivalents.

Research potential investments: Before investing, thoroughly research different investment options. This includes understanding the fundamental characteristics of specific investments.

Stay informed: Keep yourself updated on market trends, economic conditions, and any news that may impact your investments. Regularly review your portfolio to make adjustments based on your short and long goals, your risk tolerance, and market conditions.

How can you start investing?

You will need to have an account that will allow you to invest. We are going to cover a great list of accounts, but it is not an all-inclusive list. The accounts can be looked at primarily as two categories.

1. **Retirements accounts**: These are tax advantage accounts that have one specific goal, which is retirement. But with that comes restrictions, like max contribution amounts, penalties if you want to take money out before retirement age, etc.

   There are tax-deferred retirement accounts and tax-exempt retirement accounts, both types of investment accounts designed to help people save for retirement, but they differ in how they are taxed.

   Tax-deferred retirement accounts, like traditional IRAs and 401(k)s, allow individuals to make pre-tax contributions, meaning they can reduce their taxable income in the year they make the contribution. The money grows tax-free in the account until it is withdrawn during retirement. At that point, it is taxed as ordinary income. In other words, taxes on the contributions and the earnings are deferred until retirement.

   Tax-exempt retirement accounts, like Roth IRAs and Roth 401(k)s, allow individuals to make after-tax contributions, meaning they don't reduce their taxable income in the year they make the contribution. However, the money grows tax-free in the account, and qualified withdrawals are not taxed. This means that neither the contributions nor what was made on top of that are taxed when the money is withdrawn during retirement.

   In summary, the key difference between tax-deferred and tax-exempt retirement accounts is when taxes are paid. Tax-deferred accounts defer taxes until retirement, while tax-exempt accounts require taxes to be paid upfront but allow for tax-free withdrawals during retirement. The choice between tax-deferred and tax-exempt accounts depends on an individual's personal financial situation and tax bracket.

2. **Non-retirement accounts, such as taxable brokerage accounts**: They don't have tax advantages, but you have the freedom to take money out anytime you want.

There are a couple of more accounts that don't quite fit the two categories above.

1. **Health Savings Account (HSA)**: A tax-advantaged account that can be used for paying qualified health care expenses. One can set aside money in an HSA and withdraw it tax-free if the funds are used for qualified medical expenses, like deductibles, copayments, coinsurance, and more. A person needs to be covered by certain high-deductible health plans (HDHPs) to be able to contribute to an HSA. With HDHPs, typically, the monthly premium is lower, but you pay more health care costs out of your pocket before your insurance company starts to pay its share. The unique nature of this account it's that the money contributed can be invested.

2. **A 529 plan:** An account that provides tax advantages when utilized to cover eligible education costs for a specified beneficiary. And can be used to pay for college, K-12 tuition, apprenticeship programs, and even student loan repayments with certain limitations.

Here is a visual representation of many of these accounts.

Individual Retirement Accounts (some employers might offer payroll deduction option)	**Non-Retirement Accounts**	**Self-Employed Accounts**	**Employer-Sponsored Accounts**
Tax-Advantaged	**Taxable Accounts**	**Tax-Advantaged**	**Tax-Advantaged**
Traditional IRA	Individual brokerage account	Solo 401(k)	401(k)
Roth IRA	Joint brokerage account	SEP IRA	403(b)
Health Savings Account (HSA)	Custodial account (UTMA/UGMA)	SIMPLE IRA	457(b)
529 College Savings Plan			Thrift Savings Plan (TSP)
Coverdell Education Savings Account (ESA)			

Now that you've learned more about the stock market and discovered what that means for you specifically, you are now empowered to make smarter financial decisions to help you in your wealth-building journey and plan.

Very Next Action Steps

1. **Determine your investment strategy.**

2. **Educate yourself about investing:** Learn about different investment options such as index funds, stocks, bonds, etc. Understand the concepts of asset allocation, diversification, compound interest, and fees. Make sure you understand the stock market's basic principles and associated risks and rewards.

3. Periodically review and adjust your investment strategy to align with your short and long-term goals, your risk tolerance, and market conditions.

6.4 - Unlock the Power of Real Estate Passive Income

"Real estate investing, even on a very small scale, remains a tried and true means of building an individual's cash flow and wealth." - Robert Kiyosaki

He: "We are making so much money. Got to start saving some"

Brother: "You don't stash money under a mattress. That wouldn't do any good because of inflation. You got to invest it and invest it in real estate."

He: "Hmm, ok."

Brother: "Think about it. Real estate is a basic human need. No matter what happens in the world, people need four things to survive: food, water, air, and shelter. That's it."

I was around five years old, playing with my first Barbie doll under the table (a super luxury toy for Moldova in those times as someone had to bring it from abroad since it wasn't sold in the country) when I heard this conversation between my stepfather Alex and his brother Peter. Peter was a savvy businessman, and he built a successful metal company in the early nineties. When most people struggled to survive, the brothers were driving luxury cars and living what appeared to be a "good life." I still remember walking into my parent's bedroom one evening and seeing huge stacks of $100 bills on the dresser.

You might be wondering what happened to the brothers. The money? the company? And if they ever invested in real estate? They did buy two apartments, one for us to live in and one for Peter and his family. But that was the end of that road because they started to mismanage their money and engage in gambling, drinking, and other behaviors that, within three years, ended the company and any wealth-building they had.

Their life taught me another valuable lesson; you can be a savvy businessperson and master the skill of earning money, but if you don't know how to manage it and have a long-term wealth-building plan in place that you execute, then you will not build wealth. And, even more important, if your heart is not anchored in God to steward the blessings he has given, your wealth will never be unshakable, and just like in the "Parable of the Talents" (Matthew 25:14–30), God will take it away.

Fast forward years later, after I had moved to the U.S., I sat in a room with about twenty people, attending a free intro class to learn how to invest in real estate. I still remember the shock my brain experienced when the founder of the group on stage mentioned that it would take a five-figure payment to join the group and start the process of becoming a real estate investor.

That conversation about not putting money under your mattress but investing it in real estate stuck with me and eventually made it full circle in my life when I was shaking and terrified to give every penny I had, to join the program and start investing in real estate. Looking back at everything I had done and made in real estate, five figures was just a drop in the bucket.

Let's talk about how real estate and generating passive income can be game-changers when building long-term wealth. This asset class is like a triple threat — it has tangible value, income, and some sweet tax perks due to depreciation. So, buckle up as we dive into why investing in real estate is valuable and how to tap into this asset class.

The Real Deal with Real Estate Investing

Real estate investing is a standout option, and there are some key reasons why:

Tangible Assets: We're talking about something you can touch, feel, and experience in real life. That tangibility gives you a sense of security and control because you can directly influence the property's condition and management to maximize its value.

Income Generation: Real estate investments can generate steady passive income through rental payments. Which helps cover expenses, pay down debt, and generate a profit, to help you support your lifestyle and long-term financial goals.

Appreciation Potential: Over time, property values tend to rise, thanks to factors like inflation, population growth, and housing demand. So, real estate investments can appreciate, boosting your net worth and overall wealth.

Leverage: Real estate investing lets you leverage borrowed funds to purchase properties, magnifying your returns and wealth-building potential. Using debt strategically allows you to acquire more assets and grow your portfolio faster.

Tax Advantages: Real estate investments have many tax benefits, like depreciation deductions, 1031 exchanges, and mortgage interest deductions. These tax savings can seriously enhance your investment returns and overall financial well-being.

Unlocking the Power of Real Estate Passive Income

You need to know the different strategies and approaches to make the most out of real estate investing for passive income. Let's check out some popular methods for generating passive income through real estate investments:

Buy-and-Hold: This long-term investment strategy involves buying properties and holding them for an extended period to benefit from appreciation, rental income, and tax advantages. With the buy-and-hold approach, investors typically focus on acquiring well-located properties with strong cash flow potential.

House Hacking: This is a clever way to buy a multi-unit property, live in one unit, and rent out the rest. The rental income from the rest of the units helps cover your mortgage and expenses, letting you sometimes live rent-free, depending on the investment property, while building equity in the property.

Turnkey Rentals: Turnkey rental properties are fully renovated and often come with property management services in place, making them super attractive for passive income-seeking investors. These properties allow you to start generating rental income immediately without the hassle of renovations or finding tenants.

Real Estate Investment Trusts (REITs): As we covered before, REITs own and manage income-producing real estate assets. By investing in REITs, you can gain exposure to the real estate market and earn passive income through dividends without the need to manage properties directly.

Real Estate Syndications: Syndications pool investors' funds to acquire larger commercial properties, like apartment buildings, office complexes, or retail centers. As a passive investor in syndication, you get a share of the rental income and property appreciation without property management responsibilities.

Why Does Real Estate Matter in Your Investment Portfolio?

Including real estate in your investment portfolio offers many benefits that can boost your long-term wealth-building strategy:

Diversification: By adding real estate investments to the investment portfolio, investors can spread risk across different asset classes and protect their wealth from market fluctuations.

Inflation Hedge: Real estate investments can safeguard against rising prices, as both real estate values and income typically rise with the cost of living. This helps preserve your purchasing power and protect your wealth from the eroding effects of inflation.

Wealth Preservation: Real estate investments, particularly those generating consistent rental income, can help preserve your wealth by providing steady cash flow to support your lifestyle and financial goals.

Generational Wealth: Real estate investments can be passed down through generations, creating a legacy of wealth and financial security for your family.

Financial Independence: The passive income generated from real estate investments can help you achieve financial independence or freedom, freeing you from the need to work and allowing you to pursue your passions, travel, and enjoy life on your terms.

Maximizing the Benefits of Real Estate Investing

To make the most of real estate investing for passive income and long-term wealth, consider the following best practices:

Educate Yourself: Investing in your knowledge and taking action is very powerful in real estate investing. Take the time to learn about different investment strategies, property types, and market trends to make informed decisions and maximize your returns.

Build a Strong Team: Surround yourself with a team of experienced professionals, including a real estate agent, property manager, attorney, and accountant. Their expertise can help handle real estate investing complexities and ensure your success.

Focus on Cash Flow: Prioritize properties with strong cash flow potential to generate consistent passive income and support your financial goals.

Invest for the Long Term: Adopt a long-term mindset when investing in real estate. By focusing on long-term appreciation and cash flow, you can weather short-term market fluctuations and build lasting wealth.

Stay Disciplined: Stick to your investment criteria and resist the temptation to chase “hot” deals or speculative opportunities. Maximize returns and minimize risk by maintaining discipline and adhering to sound investment principles.

Do You Need a Mountain of Cash to Dive into Real Estate Investing?

You might think that you need a huge pile of money to kick off your real estate investing journey, right? Well, guess what? That’s far from the truth! While having some capital in your pocket can undoubtedly give you a leg up, there are many strategies and financing options to help you break into the real estate market without breaking the bank. Let's dive into some smart ways to invest in real estate without a massive bank account.

Using Other People's Money

In real estate investing, one of the best-kept secrets is tapping into the power of other people's money (OPM) to finance your investments. OPM can come in all shapes and sizes, like bank, private, or hard money loans. Using OPM, you can get properties without investing much of your cash, increasing your return on investment (ROI) and letting you grow your portfolio faster.

Teaming Up with Others

Real estate partnerships can be a great way for aspiring investors with limited cash to make their mark on the market. By joining forces with someone who has the financial resources, you can chip in your work, time, and effort — often called "sweat equity" — to the deal. This way, you and your partner benefit from the investment while keeping risks low.

To find potential partners, get out there and mingle with local real estate investors, attend conferences, or join social media groups and online forums about real estate investing. The key is cultivating relationships and showing your value to potential partners, highlighting your skills and value.

Asking the Winning Questions

Instead of wondering, *How on earth can I invest in real estate with hardly any money?* shift your mindset and ask yourself, *Who can I team up with? Who's got the cash, and how can I put my sweat equity into the deal?* By focusing on teamwork and creative problem-solving, you'll unlock new possibilities and opportunities for investment.

Seller Financing

Another option for investing in real estate without emptying your pockets is seller financing. Here, the property seller plays the role of the lender, providing financing for you, the buyer. You then repay the loan, usually with interest, over a set term. Seller financing can be super attractive for investors with limited funds, as it often needs a smaller down payment and might have more flexible terms than traditional bank loans.

Crowdfunding

Real estate crowdfunding platforms have become popular for investors with limited cash to enter the real estate market. These platforms gather funds from multiple investors to finance real estate projects, allowing you to invest in a portion of a property or a diversified portfolio of properties with relatively small amounts of money.

While it's true that having a considerable amount of capital can make it easier to invest in real estate, it's not a must-have. By leveraging other people's money, partnering with like-minded investors, and exploring creative financing options, you can jump into the real estate market and start building long-term wealth without being a millionaire.

Remember to think outside the box, ask the right questions, and be open to collaboration. This mindset will open doors and opportunities in the world of real estate investing.

Is Real Estate a Risky Business?

When it comes to investing, every asset class has its fair share of risks, and real estate is no different. But here's the thing: the level of risk tied to real estate investments can swing wildly, depending on factors like the type of property, location, market conditions, and investment strategy. It's important to understand the risks and implement strategies to keep them in check to boost your chances of success.

Let's dig deeper into some of the risks that come with real estate investing and how you can handle them like a pro.

Market Risk

Real estate markets are swayed by many factors, including the economy, job growth, and population trends. As a result, property values and rental demand can see-saw, affecting your investment returns. To tackle market risk, focus on properties in prime locations with strong long-term fundamentals, like solid job markets, diversified economies, and growing populations. Also, keep up with market trends and be ready to switch up your investment strategy as needed to ride the market waves more effectively.

Liquidity Risk

Here's the thing about real estate: it's not a highly liquid asset like stocks and bonds. That means it can take a while to sell a property when you need to get your hands on some cash. To deal with liquidity risk, consider building an emergency fund to cover unexpected expenses and maintain a diversified investment portfolio with more liquid assets.

Tenant Risk

Tenant-related risks, such as empty properties, rent dodgers, and property damage, can dent your rental income and investment returns. To keep tenant risk at bay, put a solid tenant screening process in place to pick top-notch, dependable renters. Another option is to have a property management company handle tenant relations and daily property management tasks, ensuring your investment stays in tip-top shape, and your tenants are happy campers.

Financing Risk

Real estate investing often means using borrowed funds to buy properties, which exposes you to financing risk. To keep financing risk in check, avoid over-leveraging your investments and maintain a conservative debt-to-equity ratio. Also, work with reputable lenders, closely examine loan terms, and ensure your property's cash flow can comfortably cover debt service and other expenses.

Maintenance and Repair Risk

As a property owner, you must take care of ongoing maintenance and repairs, which can eat into your time and money. To tackle this risk, set aside money for regular maintenance and repairs and stash funds for unexpected expenses. On top of that, invest in properties in good shape, conduct thorough property inspections, and deal with maintenance issues ASAP to prevent costly surprises down the road.

Real estate investing does come with its fair share of risks, but you can manage them effectively with careful planning, due diligence, and a disciplined investment approach. By getting to grips with the risks tied to real estate investing and putting strategies in place to keep them in check, you can up your chances of success and build long-term wealth through this asset class. Remember, knowledge coupled with action is power when it comes to investing — stay informed, stay flexible, and be prepared to adapt as the market and your investment needs change.

Very Next Action Steps

1. **Educate yourself on real estate investing strategies:** Start by learning about different investment strategies, property types, and market trends to make informed decisions and maximize your

returns. Attend seminars, read books and articles, and join online forums to increase your knowledge.

2. **Build a diverse investment portfolio:** Consider including real estate investments in your overall portfolio to spread your risk among different asset classes and protect your wealth from market fluctuations. Focus on properties with strong cash flow potential, prime locations, and long-term appreciation.

3. **Leverage partnerships and alternative financing:** Explore partnerships with like-minded investors and consider alternative financing options, such as seller financing or crowdfunding, to enter the real estate market without a large initial investment. This can help you grow your portfolio faster and build long-term wealth.

CHAPTER 7

Embracing the Wealthy Life Plan

7.1- Estate Planning: Secure Your Legacy Like the Wealthy

"The greatest gift you can leave your loved ones is a well-crafted estate plan that preserves your legacy and ensures a smooth transition of your assets." - Deborah L. Jacobs

We've talked about all the steps you need to take to build wealth, manage your money, and invest in your future. But now, it's time to dive into the often-overlooked part of our wealth-building journey — estate planning. Yep, we're going to discuss how to secure your legacy like the wealthy do because, let's face it, nobody wants to leave a mess behind for those they love to deal with, right?

Estate planning may seem dry and boring, but trust me, it's essential. And you know what? We will approach it in a fun, engaging, and informative way that's true to our style. So, let's talk about why estate planning matters and how you can embrace it as part of your wealthy life plan.

When it comes to building a prosperous life, it's not just about accumulating wealth for ourselves; it's also about making sure the people we love are taken care of when we're no longer around. And that, my friend, is where estate planning comes in. It's like creating a roadmap for your assets to follow once you're gone, ensuring that your hard-earned wealth benefits the people you care about the most.

I know what you might think, *I'm young and don't have much to leave behind yet. Why should I worry about estate planning now?* Well, the truth is, there's no better time to start planning than right now. Like with our finances, the sooner we start, the better prepared we'll be for the future. So, let's get into the nitty-gritty of estate planning and learn how to secure our legacies like the wealthy do.

Estate planning might invoke images of expansive mansions and the ultra-wealthy. But let me tell you, estate planning isn't just for the rich; it's something you should prioritize, regardless of your net worth.

Financial success is a two-part process: creating wealth and keeping it. Today, I want to empower you to prioritize estate planning in your financial journey so the wealth you're working so hard to accumulate doesn't vanish unexpectedly.

Before we continue, I will clarify that I'm not a lawyer, and the content in this book or resources should not be considered legal advice. That said, the information you've gathered in these pages, like your net worth and expenses, will come in handy as we delve into estate planning.

Estate planning is an intricate part of personal finance that can transform the way you and your loved ones perceive wealth and its relationship with your life. It's about creating a lasting generational legacy. Estate planning can boost your confidence in the future because you know your loved ones will be taken care of and your legacy will be preserved the way you envision. It can also help minimize taxes and probate fees and ensure your family has fewer worries when you're gone. Moreover, it can protect you if a medical situation arises, leaving you unable to care for yourself. Failing to create an estate plan can lead to unintended complications for you and your loved ones and potentially drain your wealth in various ways.

So, what exactly is an estate plan? It's a number of legal documents designed to preserve, manage, and distribute your assets. Assets can include houses, cars, stocks, 401k, IRA, life insurance, pensions, debt, and digital assets like login credentials for your online accounts. Keep in mind that *you* are your most significant asset. If you're worried about not planning things properly and ending up in a difficult situation, your peace and happiness may be compromised, affecting your daily life. Estate planning can help preserve family wealth, ensure that those you love are taken care of, and fund your children's or grandchildren's education, among other things.

The most basic document in estate planning is the Last Will & Testament. Other essential components might include, in no particular order:

- Living Trust
- Power of Attorney for Finances
- Power of Attorney for Health Care
- Medical Directive (Health Care Directive or Living Wills)

Estate planning can be handled in a couple of ways. One option is to consult with an estate planning attorney, who could be someone local to you. Another option is to do it online.

Now, let's dive deeper into the components of an estate plan, so you have a better understanding of what they entail and why they're essential.

Last Will & Testament: A Will is a legal document outlining how you would like for your assets to be distributed once you are no longer alive. It's basically a roadmap for your wealth, ensuring everything goes where it should go. Think of it as your final gift to your loved ones — a way to make sure they're taken care of and that your wishes are respected. It also names an executor to manage your estate and can include provisions for guardianship of minor children. Without a valid Will, your estate could be subject to your state's intestacy laws, which might not align with your wishes. Plus, having a Will can save your family a lot of time, stress, and money by avoiding lengthy legal battles and confusion.

Now when it comes to creating a Will, there are a few things to consider. First, you'll need to choose an executor — an individual you trust to carry out your wishes and handle the administration of your estate. This can be a family member, a professional (like a lawyer or an accountant), or a friend. Next, you'll need to outline who gets what — who inherits your assets and how they'll be distributed. This includes everything from your real estate and investment accounts to your personal belongings and family heirlooms. And finally, if you have children, you'll need to designate a guardian — someone who will care for them in the event that you and your partner are no longer around.

Once you've sorted out your Will, it's time to think about other important estate planning documents. One of these is a living Will or advance directive. This document outlines your medical preferences and end-of-life care, ensuring your wishes are respected even if you cannot communicate them yourself. Another important document is a durable power of attorney, which enables you to appoint an individual to make legal and financial decisions on your behalf if you become disabled.

Living Trust: A legal entity that holds your assets during your lifetime and distributes them upon your death. It's an excellent tool for avoiding probate, which can be time-consuming and expensive. A living trust can also provide for your care if you become incapacitated and maintain your privacy since it doesn't become a public record like a Will. There is more than one type of trust, but the most common are revocable living trusts and irrevocable trusts.

A revocable living trust is a flexible option allowing you to control your assets while alive. You can make changes to the trust, add or remove assets, and even dissolve it if needed. The key advantage of a revocable living trust is that it helps your loved ones avoid the probate process, which can be expensive, long, and public. Instead, your assets can be distributed quickly and privately to your chosen beneficiaries.

A more permanent option is the irrevocable trust. Once you've established an irrevocable trust, you cannot make changes or take back the assets. This kind of trust can help reduce estate and gift taxes, so it's frequently used for tax planning purposes. It can also provide asset protection, shielding your wealth from potential creditors or lawsuits.

Power of Attorney for Health Care: An estate planning document that allows you to appoint someone you trust who will make medical decisions on your behalf if you become disabled. It's essential to have a conversation with the person you choose as your healthcare agent to make sure they understand your wishes and are comfortable with the responsibility.

Power of Attorney for Finances: Similar to the healthcare power of attorney, this document grants someone you trust the authority to manage your financial affairs if you become disabled. This can include paying bills, managing investments, and handling other financial matters on your behalf.

Medical Directive (Health Care Directive or Living Wills): This document outlines your preferences for medical treatment if you're unable to communicate your wishes. It can provide guidance to your healthcare agent and medical professionals about the type of care you'd like to receive in specific situations, such as end-of-life care or life-sustaining treatments.

Now that you understand the essential components of an estate plan, let's explore some additional considerations to help you tailor your plan to your unique situation.

Digital assets: In today's digital age, including your online accounts in your estate plan is crucial. This can involve designating a digital executor to handle your digital assets, providing login credentials and instructions for managing or closing accounts, and specifying how you'd like your digital legacy to be handled.

Charitable giving: Giving is the ultimate fulfillment in life; through it, we truly make the world a better place. I strongly encourage you to incorporate charitable giving into your estate plan if you haven't done so already. Many wealthy individuals choose to include charitable donations in their estate plans, using their wealth to make a lasting impact on causes they care about. There are several ways to incorporate charitable giving into your estate plan, such as setting up a charitable trust, establishing a donor-advised fund, or simply leaving a portion of your assets to your chosen charity in your will.

Business succession planning: For those that own a business, it's vital to have a succession plan in place to ensure its continuity after your death. This may involve grooming a successor, setting up a buy-sell agreement, or creating a detailed plan for transferring ownership and management.

Planning for minor children: Your estate plan should include provisions for your minor children's care and financial support. This includes naming a guardian to care for them and setting up trusts to manage their inheritance until they reach a specified age.

Estate tax planning: Based on the size of your wealth and assets, you may need to consider strategies to minimize potential estate taxes. This could involve making lifetime gifts, setting up trusts, or utilizing other tax-saving techniques. It's important to reach out to a financial planner or tax professional and determine the best approach for your situation.

Life insurance: By getting life insurance, you can make sure that those you love have financial support after you're gone. It helps with things like funeral bills, any debts you leave behind, and day-to-day living expenses.

Reviewing and updating your plan: You should review and update your estate plan periodically, especially after significant life events like becoming a parent, divorce, marriage, or the death of a loved one. This ensures your plan remains aligned with your wishes and current circumstances.

When planning your estate, it's crucial to keep your beneficiaries up to date. This means regularly reviewing and updating your beneficiary on life investment accounts, retirement accounts, insurance policies, etc. Skipping this step can result in unintended consequences, such as your assets going to an ex-spouse or other individuals you no longer want to inherit your wealth.

Estate planning may seem daunting, but it's a vital part of embracing a wealthy life plan. By planning for your legacy, you're protecting your hard-earned wealth and ensuring that your loved ones are taken care of, and your values are upheld. So, no need to put it off any longer; start your estate planning journey today and secure your legacy like the wealthy do.

Building a prosperous life isn't just about accumulating wealth in the present; it's also about planning for the future and leaving a lasting legacy. By incorporating estate planning into your wealthy life plan, you're taking control of your financial destiny and creating a more secure and fulfilling future for yourself and your loved ones.

In conclusion, estate planning is a critical aspect of personal finance that can protect your wealth, provide for those you love, and ensure your legacy is preserved according to your wishes. By understanding the essential components of an estate plan and tailoring it to your unique situation, you can be at peace knowing that you've prepared for the future. So, consult with an attorney or a professional in the field of estate planning for advice that is personalized and specific to your situation and compliant with the laws, rules, and regulations to start the process and prioritize this vital aspect of your financial journey.

Very Next Action Steps

1. **Assess Your Estate Planning Needs:** Consider your current financial situation, family dynamics, and goals for your legacy. Review your assets, debts, digital accounts, insurance policies, and business interests. This assessment will help you understand what needs to be addressed in your estate plan.

2. **Create Essential Estate Planning Documents:** Consult an estate planning attorney to craft your estate planning documents.

3. **Regularly Review and Update Your Estate Plan:** Life events and changes in your financial situation may require adjustments to your estate plan. Periodically review and update your documents, beneficiary designations, and asset allocation to ensure they continue to reflect your wishes and comply with any changes in laws and regulations.

7.2 - Optimize for Greater Freedom and Less Busy Work

"The life you live tomorrow is the choice you made today."- Larisa Olteanu

Kudos to you for completing more than 90% of the work by following the steps outlined so far. You've diligently built a new wealth identity, intentionally designed your dream life, set SMART goals, and developed habits and systems. Moreover, you've put a money management system in place to track your finances and save more. You've also created an autopilot money flow and developed an investment plan. Be proud of the incredible progress you've made!

Many believe that knowledge is power, but *action* is power. Pat yourself on the back for taking the steps and completing the actions listed at the end of the sections. If you haven't done those actions yet, remember, it's not too late — go back, complete them, and witness the transformation in your life.

In order to maintain and grow your financial system, it's essential to review it annually. Also, it's important to understand that individuals, countries, and even the world go through economic cycles, so economic downturns are inevitable. Wealthy people don't panic during stock market crashes or real estate downturns; instead, they adjust, stay calm, and make calculated decisions. In fact, they often find great investment opportunities during such times.

As an investor and wealth builder, train yourself not to panic like the masses that make irrational decisions with their investments. Your personal finance plan and estate plan aren't one-and-done deals. Monitor your finances weekly, and as you gain more confidence and control over your money, switch to a monthly review. Additionally, allocate a few hours each year to review your plans in their entirety and adjust them accordingly, as things change rapidly. I've attached a checklist of things to review in the resources section below.

If you're not investing at least 10% of your income, reassess your spending and adjust it as necessary. If you're not on track to achieve financial success based on your timeline, consider starting a side hustle to generate more income.

What strategies and mindsets will help you live a more fulfilling life with the freedom to focus on what truly matters?

Let's begin with tackling the elephant in the room — busy work. You know, those tasks that seem to take up all your time and energy, leaving you feeling overwhelmed and exhausted. While some busy work is inevitable, the key to optimizing your life for greater freedom is to minimize these time-consuming tasks and make room for those things that genuinely bring you joy and fulfillment.

To start, let's take a look at the big picture. Picture your life as a canvas and imagine you're the artist. Your masterpiece will be the result of the decisions you make, the goals you set, and the time you dedicate to the things you're passionate about. But every artist needs a clear vision of what they want to create, and that's where your wealthy life plan comes in.

Your wealthy life plan isn't just about accumulating wealth and achieving financial goals. It's about living a rich, fulfilling life on your terms. So, what does that look like for you? What are your dreams, aspirations, and passions? The first step to optimizing for greater freedom is to get very clear on what you want and get anchored in your SMART goals to achieve them.

Now that you've defined your vision, it's time to turn those dreams into reality. Here's where we'll focus on eliminating busy work and creating more freedom in your life.

Prioritize and Delegate

We're all familiar with the age-old saying, "Time is money." But in our pursuit of wealth, we often forget that time is also our most valuable resource. To truly optimize your life for freedom, make sure you prioritize your time and energy on the things that align with your values and goals.

Make a list of all your daily, weekly, and monthly tasks. Then, rank them based on their importance and impact on your life. Identify which tasks can be delegated, outsourced, or even eliminated altogether.

Remember, it's ok to ask for help! Delegating tasks to others, whether it's hiring a virtual assistant, a housekeeper, or even a meal delivery service, can free up valuable time to focus on what truly matters.

Automate and Simplify

In today's fast-paced, technology-driven world, countless tools and resources are available to help you automate and simplify your life. From automating bill payments and savings contributions to utilizing productivity apps and project management tools, there are plenty of ways to streamline your busy work and create more freedom in your life.

Take advantage of these resources and incorporate them into your daily routines. By doing so, you'll not only save time but also reduce stress and increase your overall happiness.

Embrace Minimalism

Minimalism, at its core, is about living with intention and focusing on the things that truly matter. Adopting a minimalist mindset can eliminate unnecessary clutter, distractions, and commitments that consume your time and energy.

Take time to ponder the things that occupy your physical and mental space. Are they adding value to your life or weighing you down? By simplifying your surroundings and schedule, you'll create more space for the things that bring you joy and fulfillment.

Cultivate a Healthy Work-Life Balance

In order to optimize your life for greater freedom, it's important to achieve a healthy work-life balance. While it's essential to work hard and stay committed to your financial goals, it's equally important to prioritize self-care, relationships, and personal growth.

To cultivate a healthy work-life balance, set boundaries and establish routines that help you disconnect from work and focus on your personal life. Schedule regular breaks throughout your workday, dedicate time to your hobbies, and plan social activities with friends and family.

Remember, the journey to unshakable wealth isn't just about financial success; it's also about enjoying the fruits of your labor and living a fulfilling life outside of work.

Invest in Personal Growth and Development

Continuously investing in your personal growth and development is crucial for optimizing your life for greater freedom. Expanding your knowledge, skills, and experiences will unlock new opportunities for growth and success, both personally and financially.

Commit to lifelong learning by attending workshops, reading books, attending courses, listening to podcasts, and engaging with mentors and coaches. As you grow and evolve, you'll discover new passions and interests, allowing you to live a more purposeful and fulfilling life.

Design Your Ideal Lifestyle

Now that you've laid the groundwork for optimizing your life, it's time to design your ideal lifestyle. This is where you get to let your imagination run wild! What does your dream life look like? How would you love to spend your days, and who would you want to spend them with?

If your dreams don't scare you, they are not big enough. So dream big, and don't be afraid to challenge the status quo. Remember, you're the artist of your own life, and you have the power to create a masterpiece that reflects your values, passions, and aspirations.

As you design your ideal lifestyle, consider the following questions:

- What activities and experiences bring you joy and fulfillment?
- How can you incorporate more of these into your daily life?
- What are your nonnegotiables, and how can you protect them?
- How can you create a support system that empowers you to live your best life?

By answering these questions and taking actionable steps to bring your ideal lifestyle to life, you'll create a wealth plan that builds financial abundance and promotes personal fulfillment and freedom.

My friend, embracing the wealthy life plan means optimizing your life for greater freedom and less busy work. By prioritizing and delegating tasks, automating, and simplifying processes, embracing minimalism, cultivating a healthy work-life balance, investing in personal growth and development, and designing your ideal lifestyle, you'll unlock the secret roadmap to unshakable wealth and prosperity.

As you continue your journey towards mastering the art of a prosperous life, remember that "Choice" is at the heart of your success. Your choices today will shape your future, and it's up to you to decide how to live your life on your terms.

Now, go forth and create the life of your dreams! Embrace the power of choice and watch as the doors to unshakable wealth and fulfillment open before you.

Don't take my word for it...

"I know that at my age, for me to be able to retire within a reasonable time, it's going to take some effort for sure. So that's one of the reasons why I wanted to work with Lari. My long-term future was my biggest worry, but after working with her for a few months, I realized that I had a lot more things to work on. Lari's program definitely takes me out of my comfort zone for sure. But I'm realizing that I'm okay with getting out of that safety zone. I'm okay with looking outside of my own little box. You're going to be a wiser person when it comes to money after working with Lari, for sure. My hope for the future is definitely changed. There are just so many positives that have happened since I started working with her."

- Ramon P.

Very Next Action Steps

1. **Prioritize and Delegate:** Make a list of all your daily, weekly, and monthly tasks. Rank them based on their importance and impact on your life. Embrace the power of choice and identify which tasks can be delegated, outsourced, or eliminated to free up valuable time to focus on what truly matters, allowing you to live life on your terms.

2. **Automate and Simplify:** Utilize available technology, tools, and resources to automate and simplify your life. Automate bill payments, savings contributions, and incorporate productivity apps and project management tools to streamline busy work and create more freedom.

3. **Cultivate a Healthy Work-Life Balance:** Develop the wisdom to recognize the importance of a healthy work-life balance in your pursuit of unshakable wealth. Establish boundaries and routines that

nurture your personal well-being, enabling you to disconnect from work and indulge in activities that align with your values and passions. By fostering a life that encompasses both wealth and fulfillment, you master the art of living on your terms, exuding true prosperity.

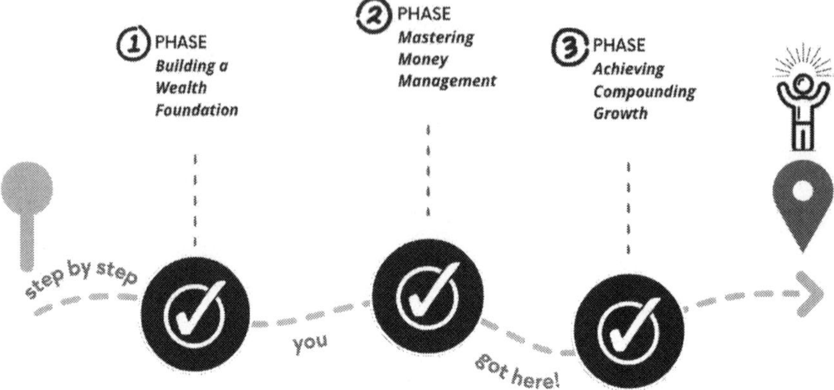
1 PHASE
Building a Wealth Foundation
2 PHASE
Mastering Money Management
3 PHASE
Achieving Compounding Growth
step by step
you
got here!

CASE STUDY

Interviews With Everyday Millionaires

Anna B.

Anna came to the U.S. with little money and worked to pay her way through school to get a bachelor's degree. She got jobs with well-known companies and built a stock market retirement portfolio and a real estate portfolio of four Airbnb properties with a high cash flow.

Anna and I had an engaging conversation about achieving abundance and prosperity in life. She had some fantastic insights to share, and we discussed several key principles that contribute to a successful and fulfilling life. We focused on prioritizing education, finding balance, setting goals, and practicing financial discipline. We also touched upon the importance of valuing quality time with loved ones.

Anna started by sharing her personal journey of transforming her financial circumstances from having very little money to building substantial wealth. She attributed her success to a combination of education, job discipline, and making wise financial decisions. Anna emphasized the significance of having assets and managing credit responsibly to avoid financial ruin.

Our conversation then turned to investments, and we shared insights about our own investment portfolios. We both agreed on the importance of diversification and taking a long-term perspective. Anna's experience in real estate investment and knowledge of the stock market added valuable insights to our discussion. We considered factors like liquidity and location when making investment decisions.

One interesting aspect that Anna highlighted was the concept of good debt versus bad debt. She explained how having mortgages on rental properties and vacation homes played a crucial role in her journey toward wealth accumulation and financial freedom. Anna's motivation for investing in real estate was to create joyful experiences and lasting memories for her family and others.

Setting goals and maintaining discipline in our pursuit emerged as another important theme in our conversation. Anna shared personal anecdotes, such as pursuing education and diligently paying off her home, to emphasize the significance of setting clear objectives. She stressed the need for consistency and perseverance, even when goals take longer than expected to achieve.

Anna provided further insights into her approach to goal-setting, explaining how she meticulously plans the necessary steps to achieve personal and professional aspirations. She highlighted the importance of taking calculated risks and not letting obstacles discourage us along the way. To illustrate these principles, she shared practical examples from her ventures in rental property management and website development.

As our conversation neared its end, Anna emphasized the essential ingredients for building a prosperous life. Alongside setting goals and taking risks, she highlighted the importance of learning from failures along the way. Anna also stressed the necessity of maintaining balance in physical, mental, and spiritual well-being while pursuing these ambitions.

Anna's emphasis on education, finding balance, setting goals, and practicing financial discipline ran through our entire conversation. Her personal experiences and practical examples provided valuable guidance for those aspiring to build wealth and lead fulfilling lives. Moreover, the importance of cherishing quality time with loved ones and maintaining holistic well-being served as integral aspects of our discussion. Reflecting on these principles, you can consider implementing them in your own journey toward a prosperous life.

Patrick T.

Patrick has severe ADD and ADHD. He had a challenging childhood, didn't know anything about money, went to college, and was in so much emotional pain that he got into binge drinking, sometimes waking up in random places with people needing to carry him home. He has since turned his life around, building a successful healthcare business in six years, which he sold for $11 million. He is currently building a second business and, in less than a year, has increased revenue from $36,000 per month to about $360,000 per month.

Patrick's story is truly remarkable. Despite facing severe ADD, a limited education, and a difficult family background, he managed to build a multimillion-dollar company, sell it, and achieve even greater success. His main message is that our circumstances don't have to define or limit our potential. Patrick firmly believes that we have the power to shape our own destiny and accomplish remarkable things.

During our conversation, Patrick shared anecdotes from his childhood, highlighting the lack of support he received from his parents. He didn't know about his ADD diagnosis back then, and his parents considered giving him Ritalin but decided against it. He also faced challenges in sports and found little support from his parents in that area as well. Despite these obstacles, Patrick's adventurous and sometimes reckless behavior with friends and his participation in sports helped him gain confidence and overcome adversity.

Patrick didn't have much financial support from his family, but he earned a college scholarship. He shared unfortunate events during his high school years, including a neck injury that ended his football season prematurely and being hit by a car driven by a girl who had a crush on him. Despite these setbacks, Patrick's resilience and determination never wavered, and he never gave up on his dream of becoming a college football player.

We also discussed Patrick's upbringing and the conversations about money within his family. His mother was a spender, loved shopping at high-end stores, while his stepmother was more frugal and preferred shopping at affordable places. His father's involvement in a nonprofit organization called Texas Jaycees exposed Patrick to successful businessmen and politicians, teaching him about hard work and the value of owning rental properties. He also learned the importance of financial stability and being cautious with investments through his father's negative experience with a bad investment.

Patrick always had the desire to start his own business, despite not knowing where to start initially. He learned his work ethic through various experiences, such as mowing lots for a home builder and engaging in political activities with his father's friend. He started his first business in his twenties, cleaning out repossessed houses, and emphasized the importance of fairness in billing. Though he faced challenges and setbacks, Patrick prioritized his children and strived for a work-life balance.

In terms of entrepreneurship, Patrick highlighted the significance of teamwork and having the right people in place for success. When he started his own healthcare company, he made sure to involve a great team of nurses, a social worker, and a chaplain as part owners. Transparency, communication, and treating employees well were values he strongly emphasized.

We also touched on managing money and planning for the future. Patrick suggested teaching kids about saving and financial responsibility early on, reflecting on his own struggles in teaching his children about finances.

Understanding credit and its impact on his financial future was another important aspect he mentioned. Despite his own difficulties with financial management, Patrick expressed hopes of guiding his son toward homeownership and better credit.

Patrick is extremely open and vulnerable in sharing his life lessons. He talked about his current business venture, turning around a failing company and expanding its patient base significantly. Although he faced frustrations with a business partner, he believed that they were starting to align with the company's vision. We emphasized the importance of perseverance, not letting our past define us, and embracing our strengths and weaknesses. Patrick also acknowledged the creativity and out-of-the-box thinking often found in individuals with ADHD, appreciating the balance brought by those who are more grounded.

Patrick's journey serves as an inspiration for overcoming adversity, embracing our potential, and striving for success. His experiences, work ethic, and determination to provide a better life for his children remind us of the power we hold to shape our own futures.

Sarah W.

Sarah grew up poor. She started working when she was 12, eventually working as an executive assistant without a college degree. She started to invest her money in her 20s and now has a sizable retirement stock market portfolio. She married an immigrant who had nothing, and they both put everything on the line in their 30s, borrowed money, and started a restaurant. They built a successful business, serving the wealthiest people in Houston, including famous people in sports and other areas.

I talked with Sarah about her upbringing and her ideas about money. She shared with me that her mom always emphasized the importance of saving money for a rainy day, even though they didn't have much. They managed to meet their basic needs, and Sarah learned from a young age about the value of money management.

Curious about her motivation to handle money responsibly, I inquired if it stemmed from her parents or early life experiences. Sara explained that she developed a sense of independence and disliked relying on others for financial support. She believed in taking care of herself and being accountable for her own finances.

Sara explained her focus on money from an early age and her confidence in her ability to handle it well. She said her humble beginnings and observing her parents' struggles drove her determination to be self-reliant and avoid financial hardships.

We explored Sara's transition from modest beginnings to pursuing opportunities in lucrative industries such as oil and gas and the medical field. She credited a mentor who believed in her abilities and encouraged her to aim high. Sara seized opportunities, sought guidance from professionals, and networked with successful individuals who fueled her ambition.

Sara takes ownership of her decisions and always strives for excellence in her work. Fear doesn't hold her back, and she remains resolute in her quest to reach the pinnacle of success. Sara is determined not to face the same financial struggles her parents experienced later in life.

Sara discussed her journey and approach to managing money and explained that during industry layoffs in oil and gas, she refrained from spending the money from her 401(k) checks. Instead, she sought advice from a financial expert and invested in stocks and Roth IRA. She planned for her retirement with a long-term perspective, seeking guidance from sources like *Time* magazine and her older siblings.

I discovered that Sara's mindset and unwavering determination, combined with networking, seeking knowledge, and making informed financial decisions, allowed her to rise above her humble beginnings and pursue successful career paths while ensuring financial stability for the future. She encourages discipline, seeking advice, and maintaining a positive attitude as fundamental elements in the pursuit of financial success.

Danny and Teresa A.

Danny began running his family food business on his own at the age of 16. Later, he invested money in a franchise and lost $200,000. He and his wife, Teresa, bounced back to build a multi-million dollar real estate portfolio.

Danny, Teresa, and I had a truly meaningful discussion about our personal journeys toward building wealth and leading prosperous lives. Danny shared his motivations, his struggles with failed restaurant businesses, and his transformative discovery of real estate and motivational books.

Danny and Teresa were hit especially hard by the challenges from their failing restaurant business, and despite being advised to file for bankruptcy, they chose a different path. They didn't want to take the easy way out, so they turned to prayer for guidance. With the support of their Christian friends and Danny's father, they made the difficult decision to close the restaurant and shifted their focus toward the real estate business. This eventually led to their remarkable success.

During our conversation, we also reflected on the influence of our parents on our journeys. Danny's parents, who started their own businesses, and Teresa's mother, a midwife, instilled in them a strong work ethic and entrepreneurial spirit. Teresa drew great inspiration from her father's 40-year commitment working with one construction company.

Danny and Teresa shared their experiences of resilience and determination. Teresa's unwavering support helped Danny turn their grocery store and real estate business around after the passing of his father. We also discussed their plans for semi-retirement, highlighting their desire to enjoy the fruits of their labor while still pursuing their entrepreneurial passions.

The topic then shifted to their real estate business, which demands continuous effort even while traveling. Danny, inspired by a motivational book, discovered that success is attainable even without a college degree. This newfound motivation propelled him to thrive in the industry. We delved into their unwavering motivation and refusal to succumb to the challenges they faced in real estate. Danny's drive to provide a better life for his family and his strong work ethic continue to fuel his determination to constantly strive for more.

Maintaining a balance between work and family life became a significant focus of our conversation. Danny and Teresa emphasized the importance of prioritizing their relationship as a couple and learning from the mistakes of their parents. They stressed the need to keep the fire and excitement alive in their relationship through date nights and engaging in various activities.

We also discussed the significance of setting goals, particularly in the realm of real estate. Danny shared his own journey of goal-setting and how his father gifted properties to his grandchildren, which Danny successfully transformed into several properties for their daughters.

Lastly, we delved into the realm of real estate investing, underscoring the importance of starting early, saving money, and maintaining integrity. Danny and Teresa stressed the benefits of diversifying one's portfolio and acknowledged the potential risks and challenges associated with investing in real estate.

Danny and Teresa's remarkable journey toward wealth and a prosperous life is inspiring. From their struggles with failed restaurant businesses to their successful endeavors in real estate, their story is one of resilience, determination, and unwavering motivation.

Lucy and George H.

George had a good corporate job making good money. His ex-wife had a horse hobby and maxed out every card and spent all their money on this habit. Eventually, they divorced, and George found himself in his 40s in debt. He met his current wife, Lucy, and they became financially literate and built 7-figures worth of wealth, mostly in the stock market.

During my interview, I had the opportunity to ask George and Lucy about their upbringing and their perspectives on money. As George shared, his father, a civil servant, instilled in him the importance of pursuing scholarships for college. Initially, George had an arrogant attitude towards work, but over time, he learned the value of adaptability and hard work.

Lucy recounted her childhood in the Soviet Union, where money was controlled by the government, and her family lived on a fixed income. Following the collapse of the Soviet Union, her family lost everything. However, through the support of family members and personal sacrifices, they were able to rebuild their lives.

George then reflected on his family's financial situation while growing up, highlighting the trust-based relationship his parents had when it came to money. They prioritized giving to the church and other charities. However, George faced his own financial struggles early in his career and marriage. Conflicting priorities between him and his ex-wife ultimately led to the failure of their marriage.

George also talked candidly about his experience of going through a divorce, which left him with nothing but a significant amount of debt. However, he found hope when he met Lucy. Together, they took classes and educated themselves on investing and financial management, working their way back from ground zero.

Lucy and George also shared their past experiences with multi-level marketing and investing. Through these ventures, they learned valuable lessons about self-discipline, planning, and prioritization. They realized the importance of selling a valuable product at a reasonable price but concluded that building a network for commission-based earnings was not the path for them.

In terms of their investment strategies, Lucy and George used to engage in complex options trading but ditched that due to the associated risks and complexity. They now focus on long-term investing rather than short-term transactions.

Throughout their financial journey, Lucy and George have emphasized their priorities, goals, and sacrifices that led them from having nothing to achieving a seven-figure net worth. They highlighted the significance of prioritizing God, family, giving back, and avoiding the trap of comparing oneself to others.

They discussed their decision to prioritize saving for retirement, investing in low-risk options, paying off debt more efficiently, and being better with their spending habits. They stressed the importance of finding a balance between frugality and enjoying life's experiences, relying on their faith to overcome financial struggles.

Lucy and I engaged in a meaningful conversation about financial management and the significance of moderation, being frugal, and finding balance in life. Additionally, we emphasized the role of faith and togetherness in achieving both financial and personal success.

My interview with George and Lucy provided valuable insights into their upbringing, financial struggles, and ultimate triumphs. Through their experiences, you can gain inspiration and guidance on topics such as adaptability, hard work, financial planning, and finding balance in life. Their story serves as a testament to the transformative power of perseverance, faith, and prioritizing what truly matters.

Renu B.

Renu is from a poor country, worked for Enron, and lost all her retirement when Enron collapsed. She started a cleaning business with $50,000 and grew it to millions.

In my conversation with Renu, we explored her remarkable journey from working at Enron to becoming an entrepreneur. We explored the significance of setting goals and how that guided her in selecting the ideal franchise to initiate her business.

Renu and her husband embarked on their entrepreneurial journey by establishing a cleaning business with specific objectives. Their goal was to break even within the first year and generate profits by the second year. Through their relentless efforts and determination, they not only achieved success but also joined the prestigious million-dollar club while investing less capital compared to other franchise owners.

Renu reflected on her path to attaining their millionaire status and shared the wise financial decisions she made along the way. These included strategic investments in the stock market and real estate. Renu also emphasized the importance of prioritizing life experiences over material possessions, a perspective deeply influenced by her upbringing in India.

She highlighted the mindset shifts she had to undergo to pave the way for personal growth and success. These transformations encompassed valuing education, practicing effective money management, handling expectations, and enhancing communication within relationships. While acknowledging past mistakes, particularly in parenting, Renu remains focused on progress and forward momentum, choosing not to dwell on setbacks.

The challenges of maintaining a harmonious balance between work and family were a focus of our discussion. Renu and I exchanged insights on the crucial role of having a support system and the mindset adjustments required to navigate the complexities of entrepreneurship. Renu underscored the importance of taking action and avoiding self-criticism.

My conversation with Renu shed light on her incredible journey, from her tenure at Enron to her emergence as a successful entrepreneur. Through her experiences, we gained valuable insights into the power of setting goals, making sound financial decisions, embracing mindset shifts, and finding equilibrium between professional and personal life. Renu's story serves as an inspiration for aspiring entrepreneurs, showcasing the rewards that come with determination, resilience, and a willingness to learn and grow.

Resources

Stanley, T. J., & Danko, W. D. (1996). The Millionaire Next Door: The Surprising Secrets of America's Wealthy.

Covey, S. R. (1989). The 7 Habits of Highly Effective People: Powerful Lessons in Personal Change.

Robbins, T. (2014). MONEY Master the Game: 7 Simple Steps to Financial Freedom.

Kiyosaki, R. T. (1997). Rich Dad, Poor Dad: What the Rich Teach Their Kids About Money That the Poor and Middle Class Do Not!

Eker, T. H. (2005). Secrets of the Millionaire Mind: Mastering the Inner Game of Wealth.

Sinek, S. (2009). Start With Why: How Great Leaders Inspire Everyone to Take Action.

Graziosi, D. (2018). Millionaire Success Habits: The Gateway to Wealth & Prosperity.

Frankl, V. E. (1946). Man's Search for Meaning.

Dweck, C. S. (2006). Mindset: The New Psychology of Success.

Duhigg, C. (2012). The Power of Habit: Why We Do What We Do in Life and Business.

Clear, J. (2018). Atomic Habits: An Easy & Proven Way to Build Good Habits & Break Bad Ones.

Fogg, B. J. (2020). Tiny Habits: The Small Changes That Change Everything.

Allen, D. (2001). Getting Things Done: The Art of Stress-Free Productivity.

Duhigg, C. (2012). The Power of Habit: Why We Do What We Do in Life and Business.

Wattles, W. D. (1910). The Science of Getting Rich.

T. Harv Eker. (2005). Secrets of the Millionaire Mind: Mastering the Inner Game of Wealth.

Jen Sincero. (2017). You Are a Badass at Making Money: Master the Mindset of Wealth.

Napoleon Hill. (1937). Think and Grow Rich.

Locke, E. A., & Latham, G. P. (2002). Building a practically useful theory of goal setting and task motivation: A 35-year odyssey. American Psychologist, 57(9), 705-717. [SMART goals]

Doran, G. T. (1981). There's a S.M.A.R.T. way to write management's goals and objectives. Management Review, 70(11), 35–36.

Bach, D. (2005). The Automatic Millionaire: A Powerful One-Step Plan to Live and Finish Rich

Kiyosaki, R. (1997). Rich Dad, Poor Dad: What the Rich Teach Their Kids About Money That the Poor and Middle Class Do Not!

Sethi, R. (2019). I Will Teach You to Be Rich.

Stanley, T. J., & Danko, W. D. (1996). The Millionaire Next Door: The Surprising Secrets of America's Wealthy Hormozi, A. (2021). $100M Offers

Jack Bogle in his book The Little Book of Common Sense Investing

https://www.investor.gov/introduction-investing/

https://www.finra.org/investors/investing/investment-products

Nolo. (n.d.). Wills, Trusts & Probate. Retrieved from https://www.nolo.com/legal-encyclopedia/wills-trusts-estates

Fidelity Investments. (n.d.). Estate planning overview. Retrieved from https://www.fidelity.com/life-events/estate-planning/overview

Charles Schwab. (n.d.). Estate Planning Basics. Retrieved from https://www.schwab.com/resource-center/insights/content/estate-planning-basics

At *unshakablewealth.com/programs*, we have programs to help you at every phase of your wealth-building journey; no matter if you are a beginner and don't know where to start with your financial success process.

To learn more about the programs and how we might be able to help you, book a call with the unshakablewealth.com team:

unshakablewealth.com/apply

URGENT PLEA!

Thank you for reading the book!

As you already know, 90% of the profits from this book go straight to orphanages and kids in need, teaching them financial literacy. Your contribution, therefore, extends far beyond a single review — you are contributing to a cause that empowers the next generation with financial knowledge, and that's a priceless gift.

Making that difference today is simple; all it takes is less than 60 seconds to leave a review. If you already left a review, from the bottom of my heart, THANK YOU! If you haven't had a chance to leave a review yet, please follow the steps below.

On audible – in the top right of your device, click on the three dots, then click rate & review and leave a few sentences about the book with a star rating.

On an e-reader or Kindle – the feature to leave a review will automatically come up when you scroll to the bottom of the book, then swipe up.

If the two options above don't work, go to the Amazon book page or wherever you bought the book and leave a review on the page.

From my heart to yours — Thank you!!!

- ***Larisa Olteanu***

Made in the USA
Las Vegas, NV
18 December 2024